MAKING
IT
HAPPEN

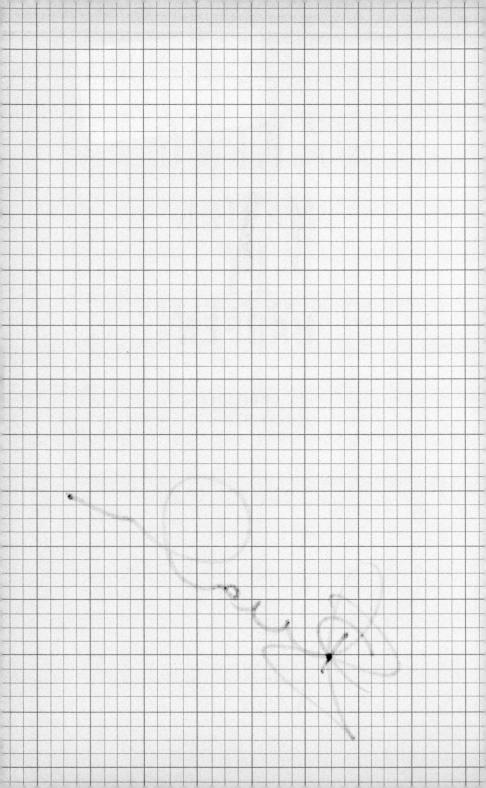

MAKING
IT
HAPPEN

Turning **GOOD IDEAS**
into **GREAT RESULTS**

Peter Sheahan

BenBella

BENBELLA BOOKS, INC.
DALLAS, TEXAS

BenBella

BenBella Books, Inc.
10300 N. Central Expressway
Suite 400
Dallas, TX 75231
benbellabooks.com
Send feedback to feedback@benbellabooks.com

Printed in the United States of America
10 9 8 7 6 5 4 3 2 1

Library of Congress Cataloging-in-Publication Data is available for this title.
ISBN 978-1-935618-45-4

Editing by Erin Kelley
Copyediting by Erin Kelley
Cover design by Faceout
Text design and composition by Pauline Neuwirth
Illustrations by Jennifer Sheahan
Printed by Berryville Graphics

Distributed by Perseus Distribution
perseusdistribution.com

To place orders through Perseus Distribution:
Tel: 800-343-4499
Fax: 800-351-5073
E-mail: orderentry@perseusbooks.com

This book is dedicated to you—I hope you have the courage to change the world. To make rain, and sell your products, services and ideas. And I hope this book will guide your journey. The world could do with a few more people with the ability to make it happen!

Peter Sheahan is the CEO of ChangeLabs. He works with leaders around the world to flip their thinking, helping them find opportunities where others cannot and to create innovative approaches to change. His clients include News Corporation, Google, Hilton Hotels, GlaxoSmithKline, Harley-Davidson, Cisco Systems and Goldman Sachs.

After a short stint as a trainee accountant, Peter worked in the hotel industry and rose to the position of general manager of a $5 million hotel business at 19. He has since established himself as a highly successful entrepreneur and CEO of two multimillion-dollar businesses.

In addition to its world-renowned thought leadership practice based in the U.S., ChangeLabs has staff in 3 countries, spread over 9 cities. ChangeLabs delivers large-scale behavioral change programs for clients which include IBM and the Commonwealth Bank of Australia.

Peter was named "Young Entrepreneur of the Year" in New South Wales, Australia, in 2003, and in 2006 he was voted by his peers as the leading keynote speaker in Australia. In 2008, he was named by the National Speakers Association (America) as one of the "25 Hottest News Speakers" in America, and one of the "25 Most Influential Speakers" in the industry.

His insights into business trends and the changing needs of customers and staff make him a regular presenter on Fox Business, as well as a guest on the ABC and BBC TV networks. In 2008, he was a featured expert in a five-part global series called *Innovations* on CNBC, and he has been written about in the *Washington Post* and *Fast Company* magazine.

The author of five books, including two bestsellers—*Generation Y* and *Flip*—he has delivered more than 2,000 presentations to over 300,000 people in 15 different countries.

He lives in Colorado with his wife, Sharon, and his two kids, Maddy and Tom.

www.petersheahan.com
www.changelabs.net

"From the creatives in the editing rooms of LA, to the chairman himself in New York, Peter Sheahan has had a profound impact on this company. He will inspire your leaders to think differently, drive innovation, and take the necessary risks to future-proof the business."

—Tiffany LaBanca, Senior Vice President, News Corporation

"Peter's sessions are always high energy, very informative, and most importantly, thought-provoking. His session on Flip opened our leaders' minds to a whole new way of thinking about our business, and their role in it."

—Shelley Holst, Talent and Organizational
Performance Manager, GlaxoSmithKline

"Peter understands not only the forces of change in the modern business landscape but also the mindset the leaders need to adopt to future-proof themselves against that change. His sessions are content rich, extremely thought-provoking and inspiring—all at the same time."

—Naomi Chavez Peters, Director, Cisco Systems, Inc.

"I find Peter to be unsurpassed in his ability to engage senior executives. Peter can draw out of your people answers to questions they did not know they had. He will even have them question the very answers they come up with. Peter is clearly a world-class educator."

—David Willis, Managing Director, Corporate Executive Board

"Brilliant! Awesome! Amazing! Inspirational! The only thing we'd do differently next time would be to book you further in advance so we have you present on the first day of our event—you set a great tone and really energize and inspire. We will have you working with BP again very soon."

—Nina Raymond, Vice President, BP

"One of the best presenters to a business audience I have ever seen. He is a master of his topic and he delivers his presentation with great style and passion, captivating the entire audience with excellent humor, appropriate anecdotes, memorable metaphors, and authentic sense of purpose."

—David C. M. Carter, Chairman, Merryck & Co.

"The thousand-plus crowd was initially skeptical of this young Australian. By the end of the presentation, they were blown away. Peter's average audience rating was 4.9 out of 5. His address was insightful, provocative, and inspiring, leaving our clients excited to embrace the changing marketplace."

—A. David Bergstein, Manager, CCH (a Wolters Kluwer business)

"Peter has done incredible work with our firm. He is able not only to energize legal partners but also to facilitate agreement between them on issues like firm values. More importantly, when they got back to the office, they did something about it. Peter's sessions create results! The quality of his work is second to none."

—Gary McDiarmid, Chief Executive Officer, Russell McVeagh

"Well-researched and highly engaging. Peter not only opened our leaders' eyes to the opportunity presented by the changing nature of the workforce but also opened their minds to new ways we can drive collaboration and innovation in the business. Our team's response was unanimous—we want him back!"

—Nicole Csabon, Human Resource Manager, Shopzilla

"Peter Sheahan is a sharp business mind. He understands the business model itself, and the role talent plays in driving its success. He will cut to the heart of what makes you a great place to work and outline the best strategies for telling the world."

—Amanda Fleming, Chief People Officer, Pizza Hut

"Peter has built an excellent reputation around the world as the leader in his field, and our partnership together has proven this to me personally. I have no hesitation recommending Peter to any business looking to understand their new customers and staff, and to future-proof their organization against the inevitable change they bring."

—Maryann Prouty, Global Program Manager, Microsoft Academy for College Hires, Microsoft Corporation

"Thank you for your thought-provoking presentation at Google's HQ in Mountain View. A number of Google staffers reached out to say how much they enjoyed it. You gave us great insight into the minds of literally hundreds of potential Googlers. For us to better understand how to motivate and develop that talent will certainly be key to our continued success."

—Sue Polo, Engineering and Operations Staffing Manager, Google

"Peter Sheahan is unquestionably cutting edge. His insights on generational change and its impact on the way we lead and develop staff is unparalleled in the marketplace. When combined with his presentation skills, for which he is very well known, these make Peter an invaluable resource to our clients' businesses.

"We had Peter present to a group of our select clients in 2008, and the overwhelming response was "How do we get him back and expose a broader cross-section of managers to his ideas and strategies?" I can confidently say Peter is a world-class expert on his topic, and a first-class presenter too. I have no problem recommending him to other American companies looking to drive innovation and leadership throughout their business."

—Karl E. Hansen, President, The Vita Companies

"Peter is known across the globe as a catalyst for change, helping executive teams to evolve their business practices and leadership philosophies in areas of generational change, customer experiences, and talent retention. His presentation was not just well-researched and genuinely insightful, it was a lot of fun as well.

"Peter brings the right balance of theatre and expertise to the platform, and he left our audience not just excited about the rest of the day but also inspired to build even more innovative cultures in the businesses they help to lead.

"Peter is a first-class presenter who will tell your audience not just what they want to hear but also what they need to hear. He walks the razor's edge as he provokes his audience to question their own beliefs and practices, yet somehow manages to have them enjoy the experience."

—Shane D. York, Conference Manager, Richmond Events

"Peter gave six great keynote addresses at Ricoh's annual "Let's Do Lunch' series. He challenged everyone, dealt with real issues and was totally engaging. The audience loved the fact they could apply what he said in their business today. We want to get him back next year!"

—Philip Henry, General Manager, Marketing, Ricoh

"Peter, I really enjoyed your training yesterday in Shanghai! Totally on point for what we are dealing with now, and especially relevant for China. I now have the tools to build a business case for employer branding thanks to your unique and powerful model for building our brand and attracting top talent."

—Laura Hamrick, Director of Staffing, Yum! Brands, China Division

"Peter, just wanted to say thank you for such a fantastic presentation you did to the Witchery/Mimco team yesterday. I have worked in retail management for the past 20 years and found your presentation so 'on trend,' interesting, and engaging. I can't believe you spoke for three hours and it still wasn't enough."

—Jude Kendall, Regional Manager, Witchery

"Peter, it is a delight working with you! Your dynamic presentations were the highlight of our professional-development sessions. Educators traveled from across the country to see you and found you to be informative, engaging, humorous, and thought-provoking. I love the way your forward-thinking comments are based on research and illustrated by facts. I do hope we have a chance to work together again."

—Kathy Schoo, Executive Director,
Australian Curriculum Studies Association

"Peter's inspirational and stimulating presentation style combined with well-researched examples ensured an amazing day of learning for all who participated in our sessions. His capacity to challenge participant biases through humorous anecdotes ensured a relaxed atmosphere and lively discussion.

"Peter is an outstanding presenter and researcher whose messages will have impact on educators not only of this generation but also of future generations."

—Jenny Lewis, Chief Executive Officer,
Australian Council for Education Leaders

"It was a pleasure to meet you at our Planning Council in Phoenix last week. On behalf of myself, and my colleagues at AECOM, may I express our sincere thanks for an excellent presentation which was right on message as far as our development towards a Great Place to Work and in particular seeking and developing our future leaders. As you would imagine, the feedback which I am sure you partly received while with us has been tremendous."

—Ken Dalton, Europe Chief Executive Officer, AECOM

"Thank you so much for two terrific sessions at our Global Summit last week in Singapore! Both your general session and the follow-up break-out session were incredibly well received and kept people talking for the remainder of the Summit. It was indeed a privilege to work with someone as prepared and flexible as you were. I certainly hope we have the opportunity to work together again."

—Cici Thompson, Vice President,
Meetings and Member Alliances, Worldwide ERC

CONTENTS

MAKING
IT
HAPPEN

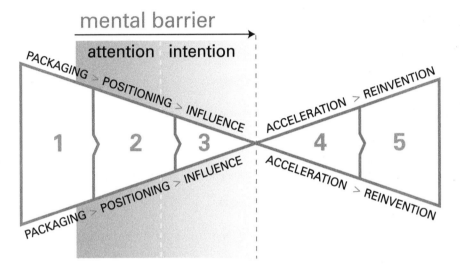

Making it happen master diagram

Introduction

SO NOW WHAT?

I HOPE THIS book will change your life.

I believe the world would be a poorer place without your ideas. No, wrong. That is not what I believe. The world is full of ideas. Everyone has them. The world does not need more ideas; it needs more people who know how to act on their ideas.

It does not matter what your idea is. Perhaps you want to start your own business. Maybe you have a brilliant new product idea for the company you work for. Maybe someone else had the idea, and you are in charge of delivering on it. You may even have the desire to start a not-for-profit organization that solves problems in the developing world. These are all good ideas. Your success, however, will not come down to whether or not you can have a good idea; it will come down to whether or not you can execute it.

That is what this book is about—turning your good ideas into great results. And it is written for anyone who has heard the call. You know what I mean by the call. Somewhere deep inside, you can sense the opportunity that is all around us. Somewhere inside, you know you were born to do something great, to achieve more than you are achieving right now.

Every year you see those same sales people rewarded for their "unbelievable numbers" or you read about these inspiring entrepreneurs that build amazing businesses from nothing in *Fortune* magazine, or you watch a TED Video presented by a social entrepreneur who is truly changing the world. And every time you see or read about such success, you know you are meant to be there too. It is meant to be you!

Well, let me tell you, there has never been a better time to turn your good ideas into great results. The turmoil unleashed by the global financial crisis, and the explosion of new regulation that has followed it, has ushered in a period of unrest. Health care reform! The spill in the Gulf! All are shifting the status quo. And it is among unrest that the opportunities for change are born.

In recent times, entire new industries have sprung up. New millionaires and billionaires are making their fortunes. "Software as a Service" and other cloud-based solutions. An explosion of social networks and the emergence of Apps and the economy that has been built around them. And that is to say nothing of the growing commitment to social responsibility that is giving birth to new fields of expertise, providing the space for innovative ideas to flourish, and with it communities are being changed for the better. There is opportunity everywhere you look.

And with opportunity comes responsibility. You have a

2

responsibility to be great. You do! The world needs you to take your ideas and make them real. It needs you to create an outlet for your gifts and talents. By doing this, you will become the very entrepreneurs, company leaders, rain-makers, and socialpreneurs who will define the next decade on the planet. You will become the people we look to, to guide our way of life and our way of doing business. You will get to play a part in building a new world and redefin-ing what it means to be a citizen of the globe.

You know you want to. You have all these ideas and desires swirling about in your head. I know you do. You wouldn't pick up a book like this if you didn't. And I know you have heard the call. Will you answer it? Are you going to leave your current organization better than when you arrived? Are you going to start your own busi-ness? What about your social movement? Are the next five years of your life going to be worth talking about? What will you tell your children, and your children's chil-dren, about your life? Will they be proud? Will they want to retell your story? Will your life be an example of what is possible?

This book is not for everyone. It is not for those of us who are not yet convinced we have the ability to do some-thing significant. It is not for those of us happy to play small and live uneventful lives. It is for the adventurous. It is for those who have read enough self-help books to sink a small ship and are sick of thinking about what they are going to do. It is for those who are asking themselves, "So now what?" It is a call to action for all the heroes and heroines among us, a guide to transforming the ideas in our heads, and the passion and desire that underpins

3

them, into tangible, valuable results. It is a step-by-step approach to making it happen!

There are five competencies you need to master if you are going to successfully and consistently act on your ideas. They are Packaging, Positioning, Influence, Acceleration, and Reinvention. They are not a mantra for meditation, they are not positive affirmations that you chant to yourself in the mirror; they are actions. You do them in the sequence laid out in the master diagram at the start of this book.

These are the very competencies that determine whether you will become one of the people who know how to make things happen, instead of one of the people who don't. They are what separates the doers from the talkers and the haves from the have-nots.

I'm going to explain what each one is, how and when they go together, and why everyone who really makes things happen uses them, whether they know it or not.

1. **Packaging**: Taking your idea and transforming it into something you can sell, something you can offer to the marketplace.
2. **Positioning:** Aligning your offer to a market need, even if you have to move the market.
3. **Influence:** Convincing the buyer that he or she needs it from you! And getting the buyer to part with precious time, money and energy.
4. **Acceleration:** Getting the most out of the opportunity you have created and increasing the demand for what you have to offer.
5. **Reinvention:** Taking your brand and expertise and opening up entirely new opportunities.

4

Let me describe the process. **Packaging** takes your broad idea and starts to narrow it down. It turns your idea into a genuine commercial offer, something that a buyer might be interested in. Through an investment of imagination and some courageous action, you will be able to take what is most likely an abstract desire at this point and language it as a specific commercial offer.

You may have this image in your head that "packaging" relates to an actual physical product. These days, however, many "products" are not physical at all. The point of packaging is to be able to communicate your idea in such a way that the person you are trying to "sell" to can say, "Yeah, I would totally buy that." As you will discover, one of the reasons for ideas never getting off the ground is that we fail to transform them from something we want and understand into something others want and understand.

But this is not enough. The barriers between you and the buyers in the market are so thick, be it multiple PAs, withheld email addresses or literally a security detail preventing you from getting access to the buyer, that any old commercial proposition won't do. You need to develop your offer in such a way that it gets on the radar of the buyers you are trying to influence. This is called Positioning. It takes a commercial proposition that is still too broad and focuses it like a laser beam onto the weakest area of the buyers' physical and mental barriers, the weakness being what the market is compelled to engage with at the time. **Positioning** will help you align your offer with a compelling market need.

Once you are on the radar, or, as we will later call it, the mental menu, of the buyer, you now need to make the

5

sale. You need to realize that not everyone who gets onto the buyer's radar goes away with baskets full of cash. Many more leave with nothing but the regret of not being able to do the deal. You have to close the deal. This is where the ability to influence and mobilize people into action becomes vital. Put simply, you need to convince the buyer that you are the right person to buy from and spur him or her into action. You do this through **Influence**.

So you have finally cracked a buyer, and you have some initial support for your idea. Now is the time to get more buyers, with the same or less effort—or, perhaps, to sell more to the buyer you already have. This is called leverage. If you can get one person to buy into your idea, why not get hundreds, thousands or even millions to buy into it? The good news is you have already done the hardest part. You are now accepted by the buyer, and you have his or her trust. Acceleration will show you how you can leverage that trust to make an even bigger impact. It seems crazy, but the first sale, the first donation, the first vote is always the hardest to get. You are at what is now popularly called a tipping point. You have the chance to take something good and make it great. **Acceleration** will show you how.

And finally, buyers, thankfully for you, have more than one hot button. In other words, once you have satisfied one of their needs—and remember there could be thousands of customers, donors, supporters at this stage—they trust you to satisfy other needs. In fact, they will seek you out, knowing that precious few people with whom they interact day to day actually execute and deliver on the value they promised. At this point, you are on the right

6

side of the mental barrier, which means you are in the circle of trust. This creates an opportunity to expand what you do, build new businesses and sell more products. Plus, you now know how to make it happen, so why not take that knowledge and apply it to some of the other ideas swirling around in that head of yours? This kind of opportunity does not come about through just luck and serendipity; it is best brought about through the fifth competency, **Reinvention**.

So let me say this before we embark on our journey: you have been called to do this and you deserve massive success. This book will answer the inevitable question we all ask when we are coming to the realization that we can do more than we are doing right now. This book is your answer to, "So now what?"

You can make it happen, you should make it happen and you are going to love making it happen. Enough said. Let's go now and make it happen!

7

COMPETENCY 1

PACKAGING

PACKAGING TURNS YOUR ASPIRATION INTO A COMMERCIAL OFFER

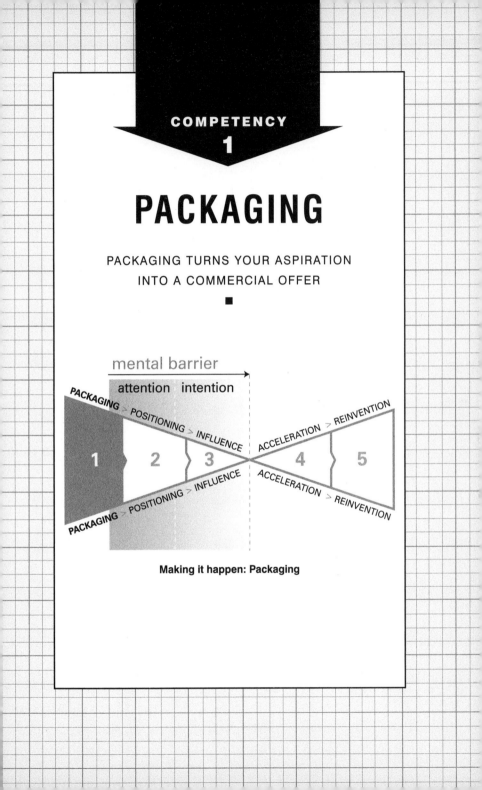

Making it happen: Packaging

THE WAY
THE WORLD
REALLY WORKS

WHY DID YOU buy this book? Tell the truth!

There is something you want, isn't there? More success? More money? Greater impact? More control? And you want it enough to part with your time, money and energy for some insight into how to make it a reality.

Don't fret; this is a good thing. It is here, in this desire, that your ideas are born. The problem is that when they are born, they are merely aspirations. And this is the first mistake we make on the journey of transforming our ideas into results. We think too much about what we want and not enough about what we have to offer others that will give them what they want.

The problem with aspirations is that you can't sell them.

No one gets up in the morning wanting to transform *your* idea into results. They are too busy trying to solve their *own* problems and make their own ideas a reality. Therefore, in order to get what you want you need to package your idea in such a way that engaging with it also makes buyers think they are getting what they want.

Now, I know all this talk about selling and offers and packaging can make the less business minded of us a little uncomfortable. Or perhaps it feels disingenuous, like politicking—or, as I once heard it called, "game-playing." Well, in the spirit of honesty, let me say this: it is a game—a massive game. Now, you don't have to like the game, but you had better be prepared to play it if you want to make it happen.

Life is one big game—a complex political landscape that surrounds all organizations and markets today. Power plays, buzzwords, budget constraints, on message, off message, on strategy, off strategy. Knowing how to package your idea in such a way that it appeals to people in the game is a big step on the road to turning your idea into reality. No one is above the game! If you want to make things happen, you will need to give people what they want: money, votes, influence. And you will need to convince them that your idea can give them these things. And, in the game, people buy offers not aspirations.

I can hear you getting worked up already. "It shouldn't be this way. It shouldn't be about votes, or power, or making more money." Well, sorry to disappoint you but the world does not work that way. Now, the good news is that more and more people are valuing more than the basic currencies that dominate our life. There are people who will spend serious money for a greater sense of meaning, or to contribute to the greater good.

The yoga industry is evidence of that—it is worth more than $3 billion per year. Why? Because people feel it gives them a sense of balance and meaning in their lives. There are companies such as the Commonwealth Bank of Australia committing millions to improving the financial skills and knowledge of the next generation. And foundations such as the Bill and Melinda Gates Foundations dedicated to social change. I know personally of large government grants being handed out around the world to solve issues of social importance such as unemployment, racial intolerance and shortfalls in education.

> **In the game, people buy offers not aspirations.**

In other words, your idea does not need to be based on money and personal gain, but it will ultimately be based on some sort of exchange.

Or, said differently again, everything is a market. Understanding this and three other principles will underpin your mastery of the first competency, Packaging. You must always bear in mind:

1. Everything is a market.
2. You are always the seller.
3. The market is oversupplied.
4. Markets have metrics.

EVERYTHING IS A MARKET

Whether you like to admit it or not, the world is one big marketplace: buyers and sellers coming together to exchange things of value. What you value may be money, time, energy, insight, connections or influence. And there is someone else who has it, can give it to you, or at the very least has some impact on your ability to get it. Whatever it is, they have something you want/need, and in order to get it you will need to exchange with them something that they want/need. This, my friend, is what is known as a market.

It is as simple as this: you sell something and someone buys it. Maybe you want more free time. Then you need to add more value at work in less time so your boss lets you have a more flexible schedule. You want to make more money? Then you need to work out how to be more financially valuable to more people, or at the very least learn how to charge more for the value you already bring—which as you will discover may be easier to do than you think. You want to contribute to alleviating the AIDS problem in Africa and you are hoping to influence the behavior of pharmaceutical companies so they can help you in your quest? Then you need to convince them that it is worth their while, and that it is you they should partner with (considering you are probably the tenth person this week to ask for their help).

The biggest mistake most of us make in our jobs, businesses, and even our intimate relationships is to forget we are participating in an exchange and that means it is two-way traffic. We operate in this vacuum, believing that it is all about us and our idea, when in reality it is not all about us. It is about the exchange of value.

Now this is another point over which people can get a little uncomfortable. We are so keen to deny the impact

14

money has on our lives that we openly reject anything that resembles a conversation about money being one of our primary motivators. And the problem here is that we assume markets are just about money. But look back at what I just said and you'll see that I didn't say markets were all about exchanging money, but rather about exchanging something of value.

What you crave (value) may be the opportunity to contribute. You may want to help fight malaria. You may want to raise awareness about teenagers living on the street. Or, perhaps, there is an awesome new project in another department at work, and you want to be considered for it. Or maybe you just want to sell more stuff so you can be rich. I am cool with that too. No matter what it is that you want, it is something you value. And ultimately you will need to give someone else something they value to get it.

If all this talk about markets, exchanges, and buyers and sellers is making you want to escape the "rat race" and go to work for a non-governmental or not-for-profit (NFP) organization, then you will be bitterly disappointed. Ask anyone who works in the NFP sector what the primary concern of their organization is and they will say raising money! The world is a market, we are all traders and every interaction involves some form of exchange. Embrace it, don't fight it.

And remember, in a market, people don't buy your aspiration from you; they buy theirs. Your job is to package your aspiration in a way the market values. Why? So you can sell it to them. Yes, that is right. If you want to make it happen, you need to be able to sell!

15

YOU ARE ALWAYS THE SELLER

Now that we are *au fait* with the notion that the whole world is a market, we have to become accustomed to the fact that we are always the seller.

As you know, in markets there are buyers and sellers. When it comes to your ideas and your dreams, you are the seller. And whoever has the power to assist you in turning those ideas into reality is the buyer. Perhaps you want their money. Perhaps you want their support when selling your idea to others. Perhaps you want their trust that you can perform a more senior role, or that your product works. Or maybe you want them to part with some of their time. This is a form of currency and you are exchanging something for it.

There is only one way to succeed in life: sell, sell, sell.

In return for their cash, they get a solution to a problem. In exchange for their charitable donation, they can feel warm and fuzzy inside. In return for their seed capital, they get an opportunity for exponential return on that investment. In exchange for their time, they get the opportunity to be part of a great new project, which in turn makes them feel important. It is all a form of exchange, and you will always be a seller.

Even if you are a C-level executive at some multinational company, you are selling too. Not just your ideas to your own company, but also the company's ideas to the markets it serves. Perhaps you are trying to sell their cul-

16

ture-change initiatives to existing staff. Or maybe you are selling your company's prospects to the Wall Street analysts, all the while trying to sell the idea to the board that you are the person for the job. Everyone is selling!

If we would only stop dreaming about the boat we will buy when we are rich or the life or lives we will change when we transform our idea into reality and instead start selling that idea, in a form that people will want to buy, we would at least be one step closer to making it real.

Have you heard the joke about the man who asks how to get to Carnegie Hall and is told, "Practice, practice, practice?" Well, there is only one way to succeed in life: sell, sell, sell.

THE MARKET IS OVERSUPPLIED

If everyone is selling, then the marketplace is obviously crowded. Day in, day out, buyers are being hammered by people trying to sell them something: ideas, products, services. You know yourself that you are the recipient of thousands of marketing messages and sales pitches every day. And the more powerful the buyer is, the more messages he or she will have to deal with. As such, the default position for a new idea is always "no." Buyers have built a barrier protecting them from the onslaught of people trying to sell them things. (See the Making It Happen master diagram at the start of this book.)

This barrier operates on two levels. Firstly, it protects their attention. As you will learn in the section on Positioning, we are so overloaded that we try to avoid even

17

having to pay attention to things. This is the first nut we need to crack. And, even once we have people's attention, we need to get them so interested that they are compelled to exchange more than just this initial hearing. This is the intention barrier, about which there will be more later.

As a seller, you always start on the wrong side of this barrier. Remember, no is the default position. And your job is to develop an idea and language it in a way that pierces the mental barrier of the buyer.

As a result of this overload, you will quickly find (if you haven't already) that no one really cares about you, your skills, and what you offer. That is, until you get through their barrier and make them care. Don't get despondent about it. It may not be that your idea is bad, or that you don't have the skills. As you will discover, sometimes it is just a language problem.

MARKETS HAVE METRICS

Finally, we need to accept that markets have metrics, against which the value of what we are offering will be measured. Any attempt to deny the measurability of what we offer will serve only to hinder our progress. The easier it is to measure the value we add, the easier it is to get someone to buy. We can't hide behind the purportedly intangible nature of what we do, because markets have metrics.

18

The most obvious metric is money. If what you do makes the buyer more money than he or she has had to exchange, then you have added real, measurable value. At this point, he or she would be crazy not to buy again if there is still a demand for what you are selling.

But let's consider a more complex example. Let's say you are active in your church, and your vision is to "win the lost." Now, this may not be the appropriate way to express the goal of the church, but I am using it here merely as code for "increase the size of the congregation." Seriously, even if you find this a little irreverent, the truth is that "winning the lost" can be measured by butts in the seats, and if you want your contribution to be tangible and valued, and if you want to be asked to participate again the following year (because you like the sense of meaning that comes with sharing the faith), then you had better be willing to hold yourself accountable for bums on seats. "Butts in seats" is a metric.

No one really cares about you, your skills, and what you offer. That is, until you get through their barrier and make them care.

Say it is government policy you are trying to influence. What is the measurable currency of the politician? Votes. Your issue will get on the political agenda when, and only when, it can be spun for more votes. Your idea needs to be packaged in a way that delivers more votes to the politician—it is as simple as that.

Markets measure things, and the more easily you can measure the value you bring, the more easily you can convince buyers to engage with you and your idea.

Let me say it again:

19

1. Everything is a market.
2. You are always the seller.
3. The market is oversupplied.
4. Markets have metrics.

Now that you understand the game a little better, let's turn our attention to your idea—or should I say offer—and how to make sure it is a great offer.

THE EVOLUTION
OF A GREAT IDEA

I REMEMBER, AS a kid, sitting at home listening to one of my older sisters speak passionately about starvation in Africa. It was around the time that the World Vision ads had first started to appear on our TV screens, and my teenage sister was quite understandably appalled at the plight of the African people. She was not happy. In fact, she was so worked up that she decided to stage her own strike, refusing to eat the food Mum had served up for our dinner that evening.

You can probably imagine how impressed my mum was with my sister's mini-strike. I, on the other hand, devoured the pasta she had cooked, looking sporadically at my sister, who sat arms crossed with no food on her plate. Young and uneducated as I was, I could not help but

21

think her action fruitless. Like all good brothers, I decided to mention this to my sister.

This was all she needed to launch into another monologue about the situation in Africa, and how hungry they must have been. Her not eating was her way of showing empathy for their situation.

As I disappeared, most likely to play Moon Patrol on my Apple IIe, I said to her something like, "Starving yourself won't feed anyone in Africa." I have since heard it put far more eloquently, when political adviser and author Doug Wead said, "Empty plates don't feed hungry people."

There are some very powerful lessons to be learned from this experience (not that I had any clue about them at the time—I was no Yoda!). If you were to ask my sister why she was staging a strike, her answer would have been, "Because I want to stop starvation in Africa." This is a very noble idea, but not something I can buy. I can agree with the issue, share her sorrow, but the end result will be nothing! This is key. If you really want to make it happen, you need more than just agreement; you need to get buyers to part with time, money and energy. Put differently, you need to reject acceptance.

I hate to be blunt here, but there is no point getting excited when your friends tell you that your business idea is a good one. Or even when potential clients agree that "engaging their people" is a very important issue. That is not the same as getting someone to write a check with your name on it and a few zeros following the first digit. Try this experiment. Go and talk to the most senior manager you know and say, "I have an idea. I want to work with you on making your business more connected to the community."

Then ask him or her if your idea is of interest. He or she will say yes. Now ask, "Can I have $250,000 for my outreach program?" and see if you get an answer you like.

I know how exciting it is in those early days when you are telling people about your idea to have them enthusiastically support it. The only problem is that so often this support comes because you are expressing your idea so vaguely that it is impossible to disagree with it. "I want to raise awareness of eating disorders in schools." Brilliant! "I want to invest in property so I can get rich." Right on! You see, when you express your idea as an aspiration, it is easy to support but impossible to buy.

Stop it! Stop communicating your ideas as aspirations, and break free from the addictive effects of receiving shallow compliments on them. You must reject superficial acceptance of your idea. You don't want superficial supporters for your idea. You want committed buyers.

Once you have moved on from this support-seeking behavior, you need to get to work on expressing your idea in such a way that someone can in fact engage with it as a buyer. And, in order to do this, you need to progress your idea from an aspiration into a concept, and from a concept into an offer.

23

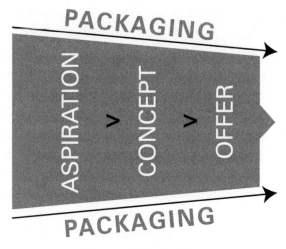

From aspiration to offer

The simplest way to explain this evolution is to show you a few examples.

ASPIRATION	CONCEPT	OFFER
"I want to fight starvation in Africa"	"I want to stage a strike to raise awareness of starvation in Africa"	"I want to stage a strike to both raise awareness of starvation in Africa and raise money for World Vision through participant sponsorships to contribute to alleviating the problem"

24

Can you see the difference? It should be clear, and you may also have picked up that this idea has already become a reality. It was started in 1971 by some students in Calgary and evolved into the 30-hour famine in 21 different countries, a 24-hour famine in the UK and a 40-hour famine in Australia. The U.S. event alone raises more than $10 million a year. It is all well and good to want to stop starvation in Africa. It is better to have a specific, executable idea for doing something about it.

Consider this hypothetical example:

ASPIRATION	CONCEPT	OFFER
"I want to work for myself"	"I want to start a retail consultancy"	"I want to sell database solutions to retailers that will help maximize average dollar sales in stores"

Again, the difference is marked. So, the question is how do we take our aspiration and transform it into a concept and then into an offer? Well, the good news is that how is also the answer. The key to getting your idea from aspiration through concept to offer is to engage in a form of Socratic questioning. Put simply, ask, "How?" (instead of why—the usual Socratic method) over and over again:

"I want to start making money working for myself."
How?
"By starting my own business."

25

How?

"Consulting to retailers."

How?

"Advising them on how to maximize average dollar sales in stores."

How?

"By developing database solutions."

How?

"By extracting information about customers that allows me to tailor their store experience in such a compelling way that they stay longer and therefore buy more each time they visit."

What I have just said might not make entire sense to you as the reader, because you are likely not a retailer and are therefore not the target buyer. Your idea does not have to be clear and compelling to everyone. But it definitely needs to be this to the buyer whom you wish to engage. Later, we will devote significant energy to understanding the "codes" of different industries and how using industry jargon is often not a bad thing, despite how much we like to poke fun at it.

So, the question is how do we take our aspiration and transform it into a concept and then into an offer?

Mark Benioff had an aspiration. To end software! In fact, he wanted it so badly that he made it the official mission of his company, Salesforce.com, in 1999 when he started it. This was his aspiration.

However, Salesforce.com did not become a powerhouse of Customer Relationship Management (CRM) technology and a pioneer of cloud-based computing by selling the "end of software." You see, even though you can buy into the idea of the end of software, you can't actually buy *it*. Technically there is no it.

Thankfully, Benioff understood the power of packaging and on the floor of his rented apartment in San Francisco he worked his aspiration into a concept—CRM solutions—and then into the solid offer of an online CRM, with a single source database, accessible anytime, from anywhere with an internet connection.

Now as a CEO of a company with staff spread all over the world, I can tell you anywhere, anytime, CRM with one set of data is a dream come true. His aspiration to end software was perfectly translated into an offer.

Salesforce.com is an example we will track through the book. It is a textbook example of "Making It Happen" and its considerable and ever-growing commercial success can act as a guide for all of wanting to turn our ideas into reality.

To give you one last example, consider the young commerce graduate who recently shared her aspiration with me and a large lecture hall. She wanted to, "inspire young people to give blood." A simple and worthy aspiration.

I asked her how.

Thankfully, she had given this some thought already and said she was considering running blood-donor events.

"How would they work and how will they attract young donors?" I asked.

"I think we could get a band to volunteer to play, and instead of selling tickets for cash we will sell them for blood. Donation is the ticket in."

27

Now she had an offer. She went on to map out in the space of less than five minutes a plan for getting the media on board, which blood banks she would target and a few cool ways to market it. Now that is an offer. Compare it with my sister's hunger strike in its ability to make a difference.

3

BUILDING A
BETTER OFFER

NOT ALL OFFERS are great offers. Just because you have done the small amount of work it takes to turn an aspiration into an offer, it does not mean that anyone will want to buy it.

There are generally three ways in which offers can fail.

1. They are too cute.
2. They lack personal investment.
3. They are untested.

THE CURSE OF CUTE

Creative does not always equal compelling.

I remember as a teenager how difficult it was to pick up girls. I was basically useless, which thankfully was a lot better than most of my friends. Still, it was not good enough. So I sought the advice of my sisters.

I have six sisters, and all of them had beautiful friends. One night, I asked one of my sisters and two of her friends what the secret to chatting up girls was. After some initial discussion about general dress and confidence, we got onto the inevitable discussion about looks. And here is where I was sure I was going wrong. I had plenty of confidence and could talk to anyone about anything. I just couldn't close the deal.

In a pathetic cry for attention, especially from my sister's friends, I sadly exclaimed that maybe I was just not good-looking enough. "No, no, of course you are. We all think you're really cute."

And there it was—that word C-U-T-E! At worst, cute means not-ugly, and at best that I am interesting in a "cuddly" kind of way. This sounds better than the alternative, but it was a death sentence when it came to dating. After some more chat, we worked out that cute is fine, but what teenage girls are really into is H-O-T. Hot is where the action is.

Now, at this point I can hear you wondering what Sheahan is doing psychoanalyzing his lack of female attention as a boy, but trust me the metaphor is apt for what we are talking about.

Too many ideas are cute, and not enough are hot. That is to say, when transposed onto the business of making it happen, too many ideas are creative, and not enough are compelling.

30

Consider the miniaturization of mobile telephones over the last decade. Smaller and smaller they got. Serious creativity (through scientific insight and design) went into creating such tiny phones. There was only one problem:

the majority of the adult population could not use them. Why? Their fingers were too big to hit the right buttons. People would marvel at the technology but buy something less advanced because it worked better.

Tiny phones were a cute idea. At first glance, people couldn't help but be fascinated. "Brilliant!" some even said. A hot idea was the innovation whereby we were able to have "small-enough" phones with full QWERTY keyboards on them, the breakthrough being that the manufacturers had meticulously modeled the shape and layout of the buttons so even large adult thumbs could quite quickly type with them. And that hot idea became the ubiquitous, although currently suffering at the hands of the Droid, iPhone, and the Blackberry. So well-designed was the size and shape of the BlackBerry, there are now forums offering tutorials that guarantee you will be able to type 50–60 words per minute on a BlackBerry using your thumbs without even looking. Now that was a hot idea. And for the previously unknown Canadian company RIM, it was a cash cow too.

If you want to create a better offer, resist the urge to get too cute by being creative and look for genuine innovation instead. As you will quickly realize, this takes a lot more work. You will need to truly invest your time and energy into the development of your offer.

INVESTING YOURSELF INTO YOUR OFFER

Do you think that Jerry Seinfeld was born funny? No one can deny the simple brilliance of the many seemingly pointless situations Seinfeld and his friends found themselves in

31

during an episode of his eponymous mega-smash sitcom. One thing is for sure, though: Seinfeld's highly developed creativity and imagination were not things he was just born with.

Jerry Seinfeld has been asked umpteen times for advice on how to become a successful comedian. Now, you would expect him to have some extraordinary story about having a tough childhood, or built-up anger, or a natural gift, but he keeps it simple. He says:

- Do the work.
- Write every day.

As simple as that!

Seinfeld is even reported to have got into a habit of setting his alarm extremely early in the morning, getting up and writing for four hours, and then going back to bed. He once shared a story in a speech to fellow comedians about how he had spent eight hours taking an eight-word sentence and making it five, as comedy is often about brevity. He was asked by a journalist once about how much practice he had done before appearing on The Tonight Show for the first time, to which he replied that he had probably delivered the three-minute segment more than a thousand times. He had honed it and honed it and honed it in front of audiences everywhere, preparing for his big TV appearance.

And herein lies the answer to the question, "What does it take to create great offers?" It takes work. Not just the "think about it while you do other things" kind of work, but the real "sit down and get it done" kind of work.

As it turns out, there is now a huge swathe of research supporting the notion that no one is born brilliant. An exceptionally well presented study is Geoff Colvin's *Talent is Overrated*. Colvin explores the research of academics such as K. Anders Ericsson and Benjamin Bloom. The key premise to their findings is that to be truly world-class, you need to systematically engage in "deliberate practice." Deliberate practice involves constantly engaging in activity that stretches your current capability beyond your comfort zone but not so far that you regress. And even more interesting is that, as a general rule, world-class performers in all fields tend to have committed at least 10,000 hours to this kind of practice.

I contend that the same applies for the development of your offer. Thinking exactly the same thing over and over again is not the same as thinking about an idea in a structured way, deliberately pushing the edges of that idea for greater application, finer detail. If the developers of the super-small telephones we mentioned briefly had spent a little more time asking themselves what it would be like to use a phone that small, they may have realized it was a creative idea that would not endure.

Brilliant musicians are not born brilliant. And brilliant ideas are not formed in some "lightning bolt" moment of clarity. You know what I am talking about. Someone claims to have been in the shower when they thought up this genius business idea that made them millions. This is a myth. It quite simply is not true. Sure, they may have gained some additional clarity in the shower, but they were working on and thinking about what underpins that idea for months and even years before the genius struck.

33

Mark Benioff of Salesforce.com has long said that the idea for Salesforce.com and the end of software had come to him on a spiritual retreat. Sure, that clarity may have come to him during his meditative state, but I would bet the billion dollars that is now Salesforce.com's market cap that his 13 years at Oracle, witnessing the frustration and challenges companies have with major software installations, had something to do with his "passion" to bring froth the end of software. If you don't already know it Oracle sells, among other things, CRM solutions. And to the credit of Salesforce.com, Oracle now has an aggressive on-demand CRM offer which sounds a lot like what Benioff has built.

To take a live example, consider this book you are reading right now. It is one thing to say, "I want to write a book;" it is a whole other thing to say what that book will be about, what the chapters are, and what they will include. And yet, as hard as getting clarity around this is (which in effect is the offer), the really difficult part is still to come, and that is to commit the words to paper.

Many an author has been held back for years—some for a lifetime—planning his or her chapters, never actually taking the next step. And, let me tell you, the greatest plans for your book rarely if ever match the end result.

At the very moment that I am writing this, it is a gorgeous Queensland morning and I have traveled away from family and friends to find the time to develop the concept for the book you are now reading. My little sabbatical has brought me to a hotel overlooking the Brisbane River with Dom Thurbon, my friend and business partner. A Brisbane CBD location for the grand total of three days is not exactly the image you conjure in your mind when someone says "writer's sabbatical," but it was all we could manage at the time. And, to tell you the truth, up till now we have hated every minute of it. I find the process of developing chapters so infuriating that it almost compares with going to the dentist. And I am not exaggerating.

Back and forth we go, throwing thoughts around only to find that they are not only not specific, useful, or executable but also just plain wrong in some cases. One moment, we think we have found an original perspective, only to then find an academic paper saying exactly the same thing in 1934. And that says nothing of the bickering. Dom is in a mood. He is like your typical academic, seeing both sides of every argument and completely unable to make up his mind. I have felt at times like breaking my laptop over his head.

And then it dawned on us: this is part of the process. This is how you take the seed of an idea and make it a great idea, one that can be packaged in such a way that it represents a compelling offer. You do the work. You spend the time on developing those thoughts, testing them, researching them, discarding them, and sometimes starting again from scratch. It is deliberate. It takes work.

So do the work! It is through this investment—doing the work—that your offer is refined and further enhanced to the point where it has become a great offer.

PUT IT TO THE TEST

You have to test your idea in conditions that resemble the real world. All the thinking, strategizing and imagination in the world will amount to nothing unless at some point you take your offer to market. It won't just offer you clarity; it will give you evidence as well, which will prove very handy later in the process of making it happen.

It may seem a little early to do this, and in truth it probably is, which is why we do it in a very measured way. I sent this manuscript to 15 different people before it went to the publisher. And even then it was edited a few times by different people before it actually went on bookshop shelves.

When a downhill skier wants to test a new speed suit, he or she does it in a wind tunnel, which accurately simulates race conditions. He doesn't try it for the first time at the Winter Olympics.

Ideas evolve tremendously when they are actually applied. In the mid-1990s, a group of chemists in Kent who were working for Pfizer developed a drug that they hoped would treat high blood pressure and heart disease. In an attempt to gain a better idea of the effectiveness of their drug, they did as all pharmaceutical companies do and ran drug trials. Despite all the promise that sildenafil—the compound—represented, it did not take long to prove that the scientists' offer was wrong. It had little or no positive effect on blood pressure or heart disease.

However, by taking the idea to market, something else became obvious. This compound would not fix your blood pressure but it would give men a pretty damn good erection. Being the smart scientists they were, they thought perhaps there was something in this and decided to patent the drug and release it to men the world over. The little blue pill they produced is called Viagra—perhaps you have heard of it.

Or what about Google? It was the outcome of Sergey Brin's ideas about data mining combined with Larry Page's belief that the importance of an academic paper could be determined by the number of citations it received. When these two got together to write a paper on their ideas and tested it at Stanford, they quickly realized they were on to something. Their action of coming together, a willingness to share their ideas and a dogged determination to test them (even if it was for a thesis at first) is what led to one of the most celebrated and wealthiest companies on earth.

Let me give you an example from my own experiences, which I have shared before in my book *Flip*. I remember when I first started my business almost a decade ago. I wanted to work with students in schools. I wanted to teach them how to make a smooth transition from school to work, to give them the inside scoop about résumés, interview skills, employment expectations, and most of all, about the changing career landscape. My initial thoughts were to deliver a full week's course to an entire year group.

The mistake was not in the concept itself, or even in its application. There was a lot of support for the content I was intending to teach, from parents and teachers alike. The problem was in the execution. It was the format of a one-week course that was wrong. Schools literally did not have the time during the school year to devote a full week to a program like this because it would mean they would not meet the mandatory number of face-to-face hours in other subjects to ensure their students were eligible to graduate. In other words, my idea was specific and useful, just not executable given the market constraints.

Not only would schools not be able to devote a full week to this but also, as I would soon discover, it would be virtually impossible to hold any group of teenagers' attention for anywhere near that long. Especially when you consider that they would not have opted in to the program in the first place.

Only through actually calling up schools and trying to sell full-week courses did I gain the clarity to know that another approach was needed. As it turned out, what they wanted were period-long, high-energy seminars with handouts that went into more detail should the students wish to do something with the information. This was pretty far from my original expression of my offer, but thankfully I tested it and an expression of it has become the extremely successful business ChangeLabs that I still own and lead today.

The real key here is to allow yourself to make mistakes and to be okay with parts of your commercial proposition being proven wrong. Get your idea out of your head and start trying it out for real. You will be amazed how much clearer things will become with some immediate feedback.

Even if you can't actually test it—for whatever reason— it is no excuse not to get started. Consider the following example. Do you like cars? I love them, and I want you to imagine that you work in the automotive industry. Imagine that the company you work for is considered one of the most conservative in the industry. Imagine you work for Lexus.

38

Toyota, and of course its subsidiary brand Lexus, has been the poster child of excellence amidst an ailing motor industry for years. Admittedly they have had their share of issues lately, some real, some media generated, but nobody can deny their dominance over the last 2 decades. The success of the company is built on a strict adherence to very detailed production plans and its unwavering commitment to quality. Now imagine you have worked there and religiously toed the company line for 26 years.

The whole time you have been there, though, from your time working in Toyota itself through to your time working on the development of the flagship LS460 for Lexus, you have had this aspiration to build a Lexus you would personally want to own. You are a little more wild at heart than the brand you work for, and you have long dreamed of building a high-performance model to compete with the swashbuckling Mercedes-Benz C-Class AMG and the BMW M3. You have tried to get your boss and your boss's boss excited by the idea, but no one wants a bar of it. Product planning, however, will not give you a flat-out no, probably out of fear that if a competitor brings out an equivalent model they will potentially lose their jobs. So they give you permission to work up your idea. But in an attempt to kill it, they give you no resources and forbid you from working on it during normal hours.

While working in the brand-development team, you go under the radar in search of a group of rogue, performance-hungry engineers. You find them, and together you build your very own skunk works. By day, you and your posse work your real jobs; by night, you get together and start developing the ultimate performance sedan.

As you can imagine, word starts to spread and other rogue engineers want to join the team. At times, you have up to 300 people working in their own time, under the

39

radar of their bosses' attention, and of their own accord to develop this car. They scour the parts of existing Lexus engines and existing internal equipment so you can build a prototype at little or no hard cost to you or the business.

Now this thing is bigger than Ben-Hur, and leadership have heard about it. Somehow, no one says anything. You are still doing your job, so leadership give you the green light, by not giving you any light at all. Only this time, you figure you have more creative license and, based on the conclusion that you really can't build this thing on your own, you go to your long-standing friends and partners at Yamaha. But you don't go to just anyone. You go to Mr. Kimura, who is instrumental in the company's Formula One engine team, and have him help develop and build your 5.0 liter V8.

You build the car, and almost three years to the day after you launched your skunk works you test it on one of the most famous racetracks in the world. The car blows your leadership team's mind, and you are launched into full-scale production.

For 26 years, you thought about it. But it took only three years from the day you decided to do something about it to turn your good idea into an extraordinary result. The day you took some action, everything changed. Your name is Yukihiko Yaguchi and your car is the Lexus IS F.

Put simply: you can't contemplate your way to greatness.

MAKING PACKAGING HAPPEN

▶ Think commercially and remember that the world is a market, it is oversupplied and you are always the seller.

▶ Reject acceptance and superficial support.

▶ Narrow your idea from an aspiration into an offer.

▶ Communicate your offer through the filter of what the buyer wants, never what you want.

▶ Don't be seduced by cute. Do the work to make your offer hot!

▶ Don't be lazy in development.

▶ Deliberately question the validity of your offer and constantly push the boundaries of your understanding of the value it represents.

▶ Apply your idea somewhere and, if possible, put it to the test in real market conditions.

▶ Start trying to sell it, then review and refine it. Repeat!

▶ Start—just start!

POSITIONING

POSITIONING ALIGNS YOUR OFFER
WITH A MARKET NEED

■

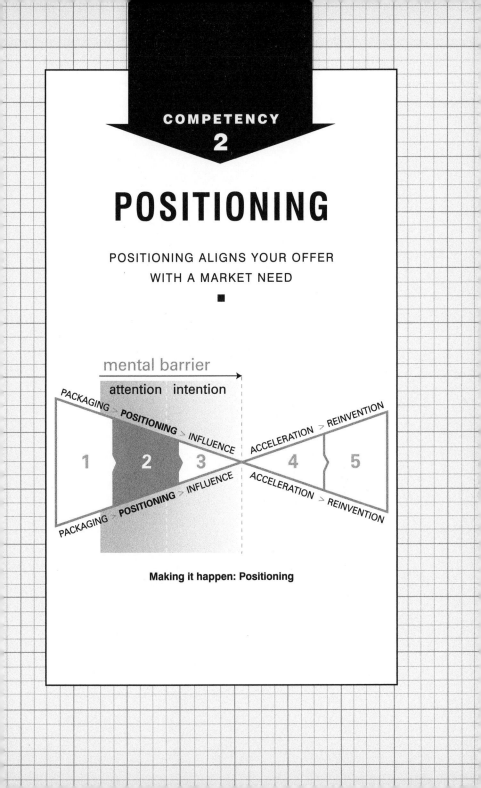

Making it happen: Positioning

THE BLUE-FLAME PRINCIPLE

OUR EXPOSURE TO new ideas, information, data, products, advertising, etc. has grown faster than our biological ability to process it. This is what I meant right up front when I said that the market is oversupplied.

Your job is to language, offer, and design your proposition in such a way that it will grab people's attention and incite some positive intention. This is what we call positioning. It is the art of taking an offer and aligning it to a market need. But I assure you it is much harder than I just made it sound.

Attention is the battleground of modern business. Getting a client's attention to inform him or her of a new service; getting a customer to view your ad on the TV about your newly released product; having your boss think about how he or she can help you develop your career; getting the analysts to see that your past does not equal your future and that your shares are undervalued; getting an investor to even listen to your business idea: these are all battles for another person's attention.

The real challenge lies in the fact that there are so many battles going on in the market that the buyer's default position has become no.

"Can I have a promotion?"

"No!"

"Would you like to switch deodorant brands?"

"No!"

"Can I have three minutes of your time?"

"No!"

"Would you like to vote for me, instead of the person you have been voting for all these years?"

"No!"

"Would you please meet with me so I can tell you my new business idea?"

"No!"

"Can I buy you a drink?"

"Yes!"

"Would you like to go out with me?"

"No!"

It is as though we have all erected a massive mental barrier (think back to the master diagram) preventing new ideas and new things from entering our minds.

We already have too much to do, too much to think about and too many decisions to make to allow anything else to enter. Our minds feel literally full. Mental energy is now what I call the third currency. We trade money, we trade time and we trade mental energy.

46

As such, you need to grab the buyers' attention and incite their intention. You see, there are actually two barriers, not one, preventing you from getting on the mental menu of the buyer.

The two barriers are:

1. The attention barrier.
2. The intention barrier.

We have talked about the attention barrier in the paragraphs above, and this barrier is why people reject new ideas outright before even taking the time to consider them. It is why we delete emails we have not even read. And it is why you can't get that appointment with the client you so desperately want.

The second battle is the battle for intention. Even if you get someone to listen, this is no guarantee that he or she is going to be compelled to engage. You might be able to force your boss to listen to your pleas for a promotion. This does not mean that he or she will want to give you one. You can show up at a trade fair and network your backside off. Again, though, this is no guarantee that anyone will want to do business with you. Your offer needs to be compelling.

This, my friends, is what positioning is. It is taking an offer and further refining it to the extent that people will want to listen and feel compelled to buy.

I want to take you back again to the master diagram at the start of the book, which clearly displays both the attention and the intention barrier. You will notice that Competency 1, Packaging, takes a broad concept and starts to narrow it down. It does so by moving from an aspiration to an offer. Positioning continues this process by shifting your attention away from the idea itself and onto the buyer, focusing in as you go.

You need to realize that the more powerful the buyer, the better your positioning will need to be. Think about it. It is easy to get a meeting with a low-level person because he or she doesn't have a lot of power. It is much harder to get a meeting with the ultimate decision-maker. This does not mean we don't go after the low-level buyer; sometimes, it is all we can do. It just means we need to be aware that the more powerful the buyer, the bigger his or her mental barrier.

When I was 14 years old, I was in a metalwork class at school. My teacher, Mr. Rodney, was a short, tanned, and athletic-looking man who insisted on wearing shorts and long socks despite it being the 1990s. He was one of the teachers whom you feared, but he was really a nice guy underneath it all. On this particular day, he stormed into class with a purpose that is reserved for teachers of the practical trades—real men, it would seem—and announced, "Today, I'm going to show you how to use an oxyacetylene torch to heat and mold metal."

He held up a long metal nozzle attached by a hose to two large tanks of some kind of gas. Then he lit the torch and a spectacular, broad orange flame leapt from this contraption. He turned a small knob and instantly it was transformed into an intense, thin blue flame.

48

"Cool, a flame-thrower!" I whispered to Macca, who was in the same class. I loved this subject.

"Which should I use, the blue flame or the orange flame?" Mr. Rodney asked.

Without taking time to think about it, I yelled back, "The orange flame. Melt the sucker," which was followed by a small laugh from my mates.

"Well, young Sheahan, how would you like to come up here and try?"

My eyes lit up at the thought of burning something, and I was out of my seat faster than you could say, "The annoying little smart-ass should keep his mouth shut from now on."

So there I was with the big orange flame, trying to burn a hole in a piece of galvanized sheet metal. Nothing happened, of course, except a large black soot mark formed on the metal.

Somewhat confused, I looked to my teacher for guidance.

"Wait a second." He turned the knob again and it was back onto the blue flame. Within seconds, the difference was obvious, as the coating started to be stripped away from the metal.

To my disappointment, my time was up. Had I continued to hold the flame in that position, it would no doubt have had a significant impact on the metal, eventually burning right through it. The teacher went on to explain that there were two primary reasons for the effectiveness of the blue flame. Firstly, and most importantly, the blue flame contained a much higher concentration of oxygen, which made it a much hotter flame. And secondly, the blue flame was more focused on a single area.

This metaphor has stuck with me ever since and I think serves as one of the most powerful lessons you will need to learn if you want to consistently make it happen. In order to "burn" through the mental barriers of the mar-

49

ket, you need to have a hot flame. Or, in other words, your proposition needs to be two things:

1. Compelling (the equivalent of more oxygen).
2. Sharp (the equivalent of a focused flame).

What I would like to do now is share with you an example of two people whose propositions are ultimately based on the same research and concept but who are getting very different results. Only one of them has the blue flame burning.

The other day, after a presentation to a group of colleagues who make their living by speaking about their ideas and experience, a man came up to me for advice. Let's call him Sam Smith. "Peter, I need your help. I don't understand why no one is interested in my area of expertise."

"What is your expertise?"

"Heart Love Transformation for business," he responded in a perfect pitch, which clearly he had practiced many times. "We call it HLT." (As with his name, I have changed this to avoid unnecessarily insulting the person upon whom this story is based.)

I had to summon all my strength not to laugh.

"For some reason, I am struggling to sell training sessions to business," he said.

"You think?" I sarcastically (and perhaps cruelly) responded.

"Huh?"

"Never mind."

He had a commercial offer—speaking and training executives on HLT—and he clearly had a passion for it.

He had thought about it and worked hard at perfecting his ideas. He was focused and had self-belief. In short, he had all the things you would expect an everyday personal-development book to teach you. The only thing he lacked was any real understanding of the market he was trying to sell to and what the buyers in it would be willing to buy. You can have an offer but if it is neither sharp nor compelling then your chances of getting any traction with it are virtually zero.

And please don't take me the wrong way. He was a good bloke, as we say down under—but that will not be enough if he wants to win the game, position his idea and turn it into reality. And again not because what he had to offer could not be intensely valuable, but because of the way he had positioned his idea. Bad positioning meant that no one would give him the time of day to explain how it could be valuable, let alone believe him when he told them how valuable it could be.

Can you imagine the head of HR going before the rest of the executive team and saying the following? "I have this great new program to roll out. I not only expect the middle management to get behind this but also would like you, the most senior people in the company, to go through the program. I think it could completely change the way we do business."

"Great, Mr. HR Director. What's the program?" says the big kahuna CEO.

"It's called Heart Love Transformation."

Now, you don't need to be a genius to know that the COO and CFO are sighing under their breath, "I can feel another group hug coming from the HR team." Mean-

51

while, the CEO is more than a little annoyed because he or she has been a big supporter of talent issues and was responsible for putting the HR director back at the executive table. And here is how that investment has been repaid: Heart Love Transformation.

In an attempt to not completely shut down the director and the initiative, the CEO asks, "So who will be delivering the program? Oh, and exactly what is Heart Love Transformation?"

"It is delivered by a local consultant called Sam Smith and it is about how business leaders can get in touch with their heart to make more intuitive decisions."

"Right. Um. Okay! Look, Mr. HR Director, it sounds like a great program but with the restructure taking place and the China expansion, perhaps a program like this might be better left until things settle down," the CEO says, knowing full well that things never settle down.

The fact that the CEO had to ask what Heart Love Transformation actually was illustrates that Sam's commercial proposition was not sharp. It was too difficult to understand from its label, and it was way wrong for the target audience.

Ironically, after some digging I found out that part of what HLT was about was people's ability to make intelligent judgments and decisions very quickly—a well-researched and reported human faculty, acceptance of which is gaining ground in business circles. In other words, humans have an innate and very finely tuned ability to make judgments based on unconscious cues.

52

If this sounds familiar, it is. This is what Malcolm Gladwell wrote about in his international bestseller *Blink*.

Only, when Gladwell did it, instead of calling it Heart Love Transformation he called it *Blink: The Power of Thinking Without Thinking*. Now, you may think that this description is still a little vague—verging on cute. And it is. The difference is that Malcolm Gladwell had what we will discover much later in the book is called "platform." He had a captive audience, and they trusted him. He is a regular and very popular columnist for *The New Yorker*, a regular on the public-speaking circuit and had already written a mega bestseller called *The Tipping Point: How Little Things Can Make a Big Difference,* which itself is a very well-positioned book title. *Blink,* for Gladwell, was a reinvention process, the fifth competency on the road to making it happen. He was not, like Sam Smith, trying to get his name out there. *Blink* was, in effect, a reposition (more on that later).

Positioning when you have no attention, no trust, and no brand is a much harder thing to do. And when you are relatively unknown, you need to focus initially almost exclusively on the buyer. To put this in the context of the buyer, Sam and his HLT were on the left side of the mental barrier (aka the bad side) and Gladwell and Blink were on the right side (aka the good side).

Heart Love Transformation might have been a great title/label/brand if he was trying to sell public workshops to the yoga-loving, Buddha-hugging, Birkenstock-wearing New Age crowd. He wasn't. He was trying to sell it to corporations, and, as it turned out, to banks in particular. Good luck with that!

Let me show you how to better position HLT for someone who is not Malcolm Gladwell, still existing on

53

the wrong side of the mental barrier, and trying to engage with finance executives. And as I do, I want you to remember something. I have not changed the essence of the offer. I have merely sharpened up its applicability and worded it in a way that is more compelling to the target market. I am merely aligning the offer to a market need.

Let's replay the conversation between the HR director and his executive team.

"I have this great new program to roll out. I not only expect the middle management to get behind this but also would like you, the most senior people in the company, to go through the program. I think it could completely change the way we do business."

"Great, Mr. HR Director. What's the program?" says the big kahuna CEO.

"Rapid and Effective Decision-Making. We are calling it the RED project for short. As you know, one of the keys to leadership success in this organization is the ability to make quality judgments fast. The market is moving faster and faster these days, and I think this could really help us to establish our competitive advantage in the market and deliver on our promise to our clients of 'knowing first.'"

"Perfect. I wish the board were more rapid and effective with their decision-making," laughs the CEO. "Who is delivering the program?"

"It is a program built on more than four decades of research into effective-decision-making frameworks. It has been gaining in popularity ever since Malcolm Gladwell, the author of *The Tipping Point*, wrote about it in his bestseller *Blink*. I have a copy of the book here for each of you, should you be interested. We have selected a local specialist, Sam Smith. He has plenty of experience, specializes in finance, and is much more cost-effective than using someone such as Gladwell."

"Sounds good. I think this executive team should be the first to be exposed to this message. Let's table it for our second-quarter executive-leaders meeting. Two hours total."

If you want to know the power of positioning, and in Malcolm Gladwell's case, quality and skill, consider that at the time I spoke to this guy, Gladwell was rumored to be getting $65,000 per presentation talking about exactly the same thing as the dude I met at the conference. It turned out that Sam was making less than that a year and was beginning to wonder why he had left his corporate post to pursue his own thing. You have to feel for Sam. There was nothing wrong with his idea; he was just positioning it all wrong for the market he was trying to sell to.

So let's move on and unpack the strategies we need to become masters at positioning. You will notice that throughout this section on Positioning, and the next competency, Influence, almost all of the strategies outlined are built on the concept of being easy for the buyer. If the world is overloaded, and the default position of the buyer is no, then the easier you make it for him or her to understand and want what you have, the better.

The easier it is to like you, justify buying from you and integrate your solution into his or her world, the more likely it is that he or she will engage. Making it easy is the key to selling to a world that does not care.

55

BEING SHARP

DO YOU RECALL the old fable about the man taking his son and donkey to market? They pass a farmer, who laughs at them for being so foolish as to not ride the donkey to make the trip easier. So the man puts his son on the donkey. Then they pass a second farmer, who scolds the son for riding while his father walks. So the man takes his son off and gets on the donkey himself. Then they pass a third farmer, who criticizes the man for riding while his son walks. So both the farmer and his son get on the donkey. A fourth farmer scolds them for overburdening the poor donkey, who already has to carry the man's goods to market. So the man and his son get off and together they pick up the donkey and carry it to market—where they are laughed at by everybody. The moral? You can never please everyone so don't try. And the same is true of business.

Without question, the number-one mistake people

make when trying to position their ideas is that they aim too broadly. They want to be everything to everybody, and end up being nothing to anybody. Bad idea!

For some reason, we have developed a fear of sharp things, and I am not just talking about knives and needles. We are all so scared that if we draw a line in the sand, make a clear and compelling statement about who we are and what we do, the very act will shut off the possibility of ever doing anything else. We are afraid to specialize. The irony is that the only way you will ever get the freedom to do all the other things you want to do is if you focus enough to cut through the mental barrier. You open up more options, not fewer, when you specialize. And freedom follows focus.

Let's return now to the example of Sam. When I first queried him on what HLT was about, he listed a whole heap of stuff, including getting in touch with your emotions, bringing your heart and not just your brain to work, emotional intelligence, staff engagement, and so on. When I asked him if he was an expert in all of these things, he was a little less confident.

I made the suggestion, as I outlined above, that he should focus on the decision-making element of what he was interested in if he wanted to engage a high-level corporate audience. His immediate, and almost instinctual, response was, "But it is not just about that. It is about so much more."

He was unwilling to narrow (or, as I would say, sharpen) his proposition out of fear it would limit his options. And the truth is, he was right, it will. But only in the short term! What we too often fail to realize is that we want to narrow the market we serve and the offering we have. By narrowing it, we can give it more energy, differentiate it more easily,

57

gain greater distinction and understanding, and begin to carve out our own place on the mental menu of the buyer.

Positioning is a form of discrimination. And all good brands, which is ultimately what we build when we turn an idea into results, discriminate. They want certain people to like them, and therefore shouldn't care if other people do not.

Now, that is not to say there are no risks. If at the start of the twentieth century you made the decision to specialize in horse-drawn transport, you may have had a few years of success but would have found quickly that the market was far more interested in cars. Only, in the early 1900s it was harder to know this than it is with a century of hindsight. The unknown, of course, is a natural source of fear. Not only are we afraid of cutting off other options, we are afraid of rendering ourselves irrelevant.

Build a bridge and get over it! Seriously, no one said making it happen would be free of risks. But surely the greatest risk of all is staying blunt and trying to appeal to everyone? We live in competitive times. There are limited buyers and an oversupply of sellers. And even if they are not selling the same thing as you are, they are still trying to get their hands on the same influence, money or job that you are and, sorry to say, there is not enough for everybody. Welcome to the dynamics of the competitive market.

Returning to Salesforce.com for a minute, consider the following remarks from their Chief Customer Officer, Jim Steele:

58

> It comes down to focus. We have to stay focused and execute. There are lots of different distractions, lots

of opportunities to go off on a tangent, but we've decided as a company to stick to what we know we're very good at. We built this CRM system starting with sales force automation at the core, and we've added to it with customer service and support, marketing, billing, invoicing, documents. Our primary focus is to make the functionality deeper and deeper on the existing footprint that we have...

By being sharp, you put a stake in the ground and declare that you are the go-to person or firm for this area. I cannot stress enough how important it is that you get this. It has been the single most powerful strategy I have employed in my professional life.

Let me share my personal experience with you.

After my initial challenge of engaging with schools, the floodgates flew open, and before I knew it I was booked back to back, delivering hundreds of presentations every year—sometimes four sessions in one day. However, this market had a price limit. The demand for my services dropped very sharply over a certain price. I could not charge more and I physically could not deliver any more sessions myself. I had tried to get other people to deliver for me—something I managed to pull off successfully some years later—but at the time I could not make the margins work.

Corporate was the obvious next target.

But what did I have to offer the corporate market? I was in my mid-20s, had never worked at a corporation for longer than the eight days I had spent on a traineeship at what was then one of the then Big Six global accounting

59

firms (followed in a close second by the one day I spent at a major British insurance company). Sure, I had run two successful hotels at a very young age, and I had a moderately successful business myself, but was the CEO of IBM or General Electric really going to care? Not likely.

So what did I know? What was my expertise? All I was really knowledgeable about were the school groups to whom I delivered my presentations—their motivations, their career aspirations and what they were looking for from their future workplaces. I had heard of my audience being called Generation Y, and I thought this sounded pretty interesting. I hired a researcher and went on a mission to find everything that had been written about Generation Y (sometimes referred to as Millennials), and in a matter of months I had everything. At the time, this was not very much. People did not seem to be talking about this group a great deal. Although they were complaining about skills shortages and the difficulty they were having trying to find loyal staff, they were not talking about it from a generational perspective.

I made some further enquiries (the action part of developing my idea), and a friend of mine in a massive global company said that the problem seemed to be with getting good young staff. "They just don't want to work as long as their older, more senior colleagues, and they are proving a very difficult group to manage," she said. I knocked on a few more doors and found the same disconnection between experienced staff and new graduates, apprentices and generally younger entrants into the workplace. The feedback I was getting was obviously generalized, but its consistency was too marked to ignore.

I had my offer. I could talk to businesses about understanding Generation Y so they could better attract, manage and retain them as customers and staff. The only problem was the research was so sparse that I would need to do my own. Thankfully, I had a database of literally tens of thousands of members of Generation Y and surveyed them like crazy. I then pulled together what was actually my fourth book (my first three were on helping students to blitz their final-year exams and make the transition from school to work) but the first I had written for the broader adult market.

I floated the rough manuscript before publishers, speaker bureaus and the few corporate folk I had met along the way. The response was consistent. No one had ever really heard about this Generation Y thing, and certainly no one was talking about it. Those who had heard of it said it would be a no-go in Australia because even if Australian companies were to start talking about it, the market would be too small to sustain such a specialized topic.

The collective suggestion was that I attempt to position myself more broadly (I would say bluntly) and write more generally about the different generations, expanding my ideas beyond engaging Generation Y to engaging talent of any age in organizations. However, claiming to be an expert on the different generations was a stretch too far for me and frankly was of no real interest to me at the time. I had not experienced what it was like to grow up in any generation other than Gen Y, so I reasoned it was unlikely I could ever build up enough expertise to go beyond it in what I was offering.

61

As for speaking more broadly about attracting and managing talent across all ages, I must admit that it felt like a very good idea. Many of the principles I was writing about, while meant in response to generational change, could be powerful engagement and retention tools for talent of all ages. So I reworked the book and called it *Talent Quest*. At one point, it was *Talent Time*, which in hindsight was a very embarrassing attempt to play on the famous Australian show *Young Talent Time*—kind of an 80's version of *American Idol* if you know what I mean. It sounds so lame now, but believe it or not, publishers were more responsive to this than to Generation Y because it had "broader" market appeal.

At the eleventh hour, I changed my mind. I figured that, as a book about talent, it would blend in with the thousands of other books available on exactly the same topic, and I would lose the one real point of difference I had— and that was my age. I was only 25 at the time. In addition to having presented hundreds of talks to members of Generation Y, surveyed tens of thousands of them through my own primary research and scoured the earth for other research that had been done, I had the added credibility of being a Gen Y-er myself. Plus, I knew that a generational change really was taking place. I had felt it in my own career, and my research only served to support the notion. I figured that people were in fact talking about this issue, but they were yet to put their finger on exactly what the source of their problem was. They had not labeled it.

Now, vent all you like at this point about the flaws of labeling entire generations and you will get no argument from me. However, there is no doubt that cultural generational differences exist, and the human brain constantly looks for new labels to categorize its problems and phenomena. Gen Y was an issue—people knew it; they just did not know what to call it. So I uncovered it, seeded it, branded it and then aggressively spread it.

I am so grateful that in the end I ignored everyone's advice and went with my original idea of writing about Generation Y alone. Moreover, I was thankful that, even at this late stage, I was able to convince the publisher I was right. Many sleepless nights later, I had retooled the book back to its original position—understanding young people and engaging them at work—and we were off.

So did it work? We published *Generation Y*, which turned out to be the first book in the world on the topic written by a member of the generation. It became a best-seller, and in the three years that followed I was paid more than $4 million to speak and consult on the topic of Generation Y. In a matter of months, other speakers were changing their positioning to include Gen Y, and marketing consultancies and HR advisory groups were doing the same. An industry was launched.

So the question is, did it limit my prospects? Did becoming the Gen Y guy, as many people started to call me, end up being a bad thing? No and no. Not even close.

Firstly, even though Gen Y is a very narrow topic, it appealed to people in almost every industry, whether they were financiers, marketers, salespeople, educators, parents or even politicians. This generation was of interest to all of these groups. And these groups had lots of conferences, read lots of books and wanted lots of advice. Being the go-to expert in this topic meant that I was able to be

63

of value to any and all industries that were dealing with this generation.

And it was not confined to Australia. I was speaking and consulting for clients in more than a dozen countries within a few years, and, as I will share with you in later chapters, I was working with them on areas that did not include Gen Y. Remember, it is about getting on the mental menu. Once you are there, with your foot firmly in the door, then and only then can you be about more. Freedom follows focus!

Freedom follows focus!

SPECIALIZATION IS NOT A DIRTY WORD

As you have probably already realized, there are two broad types of specialization:

1. Market-based specialization.
2. Category-based specialization.

Market-based specialization is where you choose a specific group of buyers and target your offer to them. You may choose to offer interior-design services to people in certain affluent suburbs. You may choose to become a financial adviser who only focuses on doctors. Or you may choose to raise funds only from the banking sector and only for your various social initiatives.

Category-based specialization would be to broaden your offer to many markets but to focus on a category. If you are the interior designer, you could serve many markets, but you focus primarily on transforming art-deco apartments. Or, if you are the financial adviser, you could choose to become an expert in self-managed superannuation regardless of the professional background of your client. Or, if you are the socialpreneur, you could focus solely on micro-finance in India but seek support from anyone willing to write a check or give their time and support, not just the banking sector.

And, of course, there is a third option. And that is to be so sharp that you focus on market and category. Returning to Sam Smith and his Heart Love Transformation, he could deliver valuable workshops on rapid and effective decision-making in the high-net-worth wealth-advisory market.

Now, don't think for a second I don't know that this still scares the life out of you. I know it does. It is the same for me. To this day, despite having had great success by being sharp, I am constantly fighting the tension of maintaining the blue flame. There are so many things I am interested in, at a deep level, that I am worried there won't be enough business if I get too sharp. This fear I have found is very normal, and it would happen whether you were in professional services or starting a restaurant. You just have to fight the intuitive urge to try to attract everyone.

In the case of Salesforce.com, our case study throughout all competencies, we already know that they were focused primarily on online CRM and sales force automation. What we have not laid out yet is their genius strategy in the early part of the 2000s where they very clearly and deliberately targeted small to medium businesses. They did this because this market was desperately underserved,

65

and because the smaller scale and lower profile of such clients/projects yielded them two distinct advantages. Firstly, it kept them under the radar allowing them to put a sizeable time and development advantage between them and their larger, pre-indentified rival, Siebel for the larger enterprise customers they wanted the most. And secondly, it meant that the bugs and errors of the system could be ironed out with companies that don't get written about in the *Wall Street Journal.*

Specialization will not only not cut off all other options open to you, it will also fast-track your progress. The more focused you are, the more skilled in your area you become, plus the easier it is to generate momentum and to differentiate yourself from everyone else.

No matter what you pick, even if it is both, understand that there is value in being narrow when you are on the left side of the mental barrier. When the buyer is ignorant of you and your offering, the sharper and more specific it is, the more it will stand out. Now, the obvious disadvantage is that the more you specialize, the smaller your target market becomes. Yes, but the smaller it is, the more focused your efforts can be and the faster you can make a name for yourself.

It is essential that you remember the concept of mental energy and that the default position of the buyer is always no. With this in mind, the strategy for breaking through the mental barrier is to be:

66

Easy to understand.
Easy to differentiate.

EASY TO UNDERSTAND

It would blow your mind to discover how often someone comes to me to talk about his or her great new idea and 30 minutes later is still trying to explain it to me. Samuel Goldwyn, the famous movie magnate, once said that if you can't write your movie on the back of a business card, then you don't have a movie.

So here is your task. Take out a business card with one blank side and write your offer on the back of it. Then hand it to someone you don't know, or who at least doesn't know your idea, and see if he or she can understand what you are trying to offer.

To be perfectly honest, in the age of Twitter and Facebook and all sorts of web-based communication, the back of the business card might be too much room. There is a new rule in web design that says on your home page you had better be able to communicate what you do in 12 syllables. Sounds simple? Try it. Try to say what you do and make sure it is obvious in 12 syllables. I personally find this very difficult.

Now take note: just because someone can understand your offer at a basic level, it does not mean they really "understand" it. Writing on the back of the business card that you do "personal training sessions" is easy to understand, but it needs to be more than this. It needs to be compelling too.

A good example of improving the above statement could be "Fun fitness sessions that fit into the timetables of busy executives." Even though I want you focusing for the moment on being easy to understand, the real power

67

will come when you combine both principles of positioning, being sharp and compelling. And "fun" and "fitting around your busy schedule" make the offer of personal training sessions more appealing.

Or how about "Fun fitness sessions in the privacy of your own home?" The privacy part would be compelling to the segment of the market who find gyms or working out in a public park somewhat embarrassing. The beauty here is not only is the offer sharper, but by being sharper it is also becoming more compelling.

This should sound a little like an "elevator pitch." The "back of a business card" idea is akin to getting your message across in the time of a typical trip in an elevator. You need to be able to quickly and clearly communicate your value in a way that people can easily understand.

In Hollywood, this pithy expression of your offer is called your logline. After the title of the movie or TV show you are pitching, you need a logline that in one or two sentences captures the idea. I once heard that the logline for *Speed* was "*Die Hard* on a bus." Here is a longer one I found on the web to describe *The Godfather*: "After a mafia kingpin is shot and badly wounded, his son abandons his dreams of leading a civilian life and joins the 'family business' to save his family from being decimated by rival mafia families."

It is much easier to do this with a movie than it is to do it about yourself and your skills and expertise. Or what about a business idea? How would you describe Starbucks? One way could be "Great coffee, any way you like it." Or, as I explored in *Flip*, "Starbucks: my third place," meaning the place you go to get away from the stress of

68

work and home. Or Virgin's airlines, in all its guises: "Cheap air travel made fun!" So what about your idea? Can you explain it on the back of a business card, in a way that is not just easy to understand but also compelling?

You may have heard this being called your value proposition or positioning statement. I would like to push you to come up with more than one. Sounds a little counter-intuitive, I know, especially after I have suggested how important it is to be sharp, but the truth is you can be very sharp and still have more than one way of stating your value.

Imagine you are a graphic designer who chooses to specialize in print. You decide you are not going to pursue web design—even though it seems like the "in thing"—and instead you are going to master your desktop-publishing skills and become an awesome print-based graphic designer. Let's now assume you have two meetings today: one on Madison Avenue with an ad agency that does a lot of newspaper advertising for its clients; the other with a small-business owner who does a new catalogue for his product range every six months.

Your positioning statement for the ad agency may be, "I do high-end newspaper advertising, with specialty expertise in small column allowances." Now, this is pretty sharp, and over time you will likely expand that offering, but showing this level of specialization allows you to stick favorably in the mind of the creative director you meet. "High end" is important because anyone using an agency obviously has a heavy investment in his or her brand, and "small column allowances" is good too, considering how people are pulling back on their newspaper advertising spending in the current climate.

69

When you meet the small-business owner, you may say, "I do print-based design, specializing in creating unique messages in tight spaces." If you think about it, this is what a catalogue is. Assuming you are an expert in print design and can do exceptional work in small layouts, you could apply that to both newspapers and catalogues with credibility. This is not being everything to everyone, but rather being one thing and working out how to spin it for different buyers. And, when you are looking for your generic positioning statement, it may read more like, "I am an expert graphic designer specializing in print." That is still pretty sharp and would capture the needs of both audiences in our above example.

Now, the real test is not whether you can understand it but whether other people can understand it. Don't be afraid to have some people cast an objective eye over your positioning. Demand that they give you their honest feedback and try to elicit it within seconds of showing it to them. In the real market, seconds is often all you have to state your value.

EASY TO DIFFERENTIATE

The second strategy for being sharp is to make you and your offer easy to differentiate from others in the marketplace. Now, depending on what you chose to focus on, you may have already gone some if not all of the way to differentiating yourself. Your specialty may be your point of difference. In this strategy, we are trying to identify and clearly communicate that point of difference.

This may at first sound like an easy thing to do, but it is generally one of the hardest. It could easily be a book on its own. How are you different? What is your X-factor? Why you and not somebody else? Why this idea and not one of the 20 others I have been pitched this week? These are big questions, and there are many different approaches to answering them.

The key is to ask yourself a further series of questions.

- How will my proposition be grouped? Who else is in that group?
- How is my product different from the other ideas in the same group?
- How is that point of difference valuable to the buyer?
- How can I make that obvious?

Let's say your idea is to start a new school. Seriously, you would be surprised how much of a trend this has become in recent decades. How will your school be grouped? Will it be with the private schools? Will it be with alternative small schools such as the Montessori schools?

How will it be different? Answers to this question might include: we care more about the kids; smaller classroom sizes; more one-on-one attention for the kids; a more progressive approach to development; a big focus on extracurricular activity and not just academia.

Now, all of these seem pretty valuable and lend themselves nicely to the idea of a new school. The problem is that these are the same things that all schools, especially the private and small alternative schools, say. Just do a

71

quick web search and look at the websites of private schools in your local area. All of their websites and marketing materials are the same. So the buyer, in this case the parent, is left asking the question: how is your school going to be different?

A good case-study comes from The IDEAL School in New York City, which was founded by an inspiring friend of mine, Michelle Smith, and some other passionate parents of children who are challenged in the predominant mode of schooling in not just New York, but indeed much of the Western world. At The IDEAL School, they fundamentally believe in meeting the needs of diverse learners in an inclusive way. They have built a phenomenal school where classrooms include kids with Down Syndrome and extremely high IQs learning from the same curriculum, at the same time with the same teachers. They are building their point of difference on the idea of inclusion. Note too, from the passage below, they also push distinctly the other elements outlined above, but there are few school in the world who take this highly personalized approach to students of all abilities, in the same classroom learning with each other.

> Inclusion as an educational practice goes beyond placing students of differing abilities in the same classroom. At The IDEAL School, our model for inclusive education includes practicing collaborative team teaching, keeping class sizes small, identifying each student's unique learning style, tailoring lessons plans, and adapting curriculum to accommodate all learners. We have two head teachers in our homerooms—a general educator and a learning specialist.

72

If you were a parent of a child with tremendous gifts and requirements not well met by traditional schooling, an integrated (inclusive) approach to the development of your child, where they are treated as a different flavor of "able" as opposed to "disabled" would be very appealing to you indeed.

You may find it interesting to know that The IDEAL School founder Michelle Smith has applied exactly the same principle of specialization to differentiate herself in the massively over-supplied world of financial planners and advisors. Michelle has built an enviable business in New York giving financial advice to wealthy women going through divorce. Fortunately, or perhaps unfortunately, there is quite a market for this. There is lots of money in New York, and lots of divorce too. Michelle brings to this market a deep understanding of the courts and divorce law, and a valuable empathy for women in what is obviously a very difficult personal time.

Her company Smith Divorce Financial Strategies Group goes as far to specify the net worth of the estates of between $2m and $30m. That is sharp and differentiated. And I would argue, as we will unpack here soon, compelling as well.

The coolest thing here is that what you are most embarrassed about and what you are often trying to hide is exactly what will differentiate you. For a time, I used to not want to appear young. I would have pictures of myself in three-piece suits, wearing a tie, pretending I was a 40-something professional who just looked 12. Yet everything I have been doing for the last decade, and much of my point of difference, has stemmed from my youth— school students were able to relate to me, and I was able

73

to carry credibility with companies when I was talking about the next generation. My relative youth is equally valued now by my clients who are seeking a more innovative approach to their business, because it allows me to see things differently and not be conditioned by decades of experience.

In other words, what I thought was a weakness was exactly what my clients liked. Have you ever heard the saying, "Your greatest strength will become your greatest weakness if taken to the extreme?" Well, what I am talking about is the reverse of that. What you perceive to be your greatest weakness may turn out to be your greatest point of difference. This may sound counterintuitive but it is extremely powerful if you can harness it.

My short-sightedness in this regard—for many years—reminds me of a great mate of mine who suffered the same disease. His name is Adam Fraser, and he has a PhD in physiology. He has spent the last few years working with executives to enhance their personal performance. You wouldn't believe it, but when he started out he used to hide the fact that he had spent a decade in science laboratories. When I asked him what he actually did in those labs, he told me stories of working with world-class athletes such as Ian Thorpe and Lenny Krayzelburg and studying high-class performers from all walks of life, testing different things about how they achieved such physical and mental domination in their sports.

I went berserk!

I said, "Dude, you need to tell people this. It makes you truly different from so many other people out there claiming to be able to offer the same advice who read about it in a Tony Robbins book."

He now goes by the nickname Dr. Adam. Needless to say, he has fully embraced his background and is prospering as a result.

You should be proud of what you have done, proud of who you are. Use it for good; don't hide from it. Please understand that sameness is your enemy. E-N-E-M-Y! Avoid it like the plague. Unless your idea is unbelievably different in itself, there is every chance that someone is already offering what you are trying to sell. Why you? Why should I buy your version of this same solution? You absolutely, positively, uncompromisingly must find a way to differentiate your offer. And if you cannot differentiate your offer, differentiate the market you are selling it to. If you can't do that, differentiate yourself, the offerer. And if you can't do that, go back to the drawing board and develop a better offer.

Ask yourself, "How am I different?"

Then ask again, "Is that really that different?"

And then consume yourself with the question, "Why would anyone care?"

And whatever you do, do not underestimate the power of differentiating.

The entire concept of professions is built on the foundation of differentiation. "I am an accountant," says something about a unique set of skills. As I have already said, the brain of the buyer will want to categorize your idea in some way. The paradox is that it will also try to find a way to identify what is unique about you. And if it can't find anything, the harsh reality is that you will not be memorable.

The stakes are high here. If you managed to get noticed and grab the attention of the buyer but you don't have a

75

sharp, differentiated offer, all your work may actually lead the buyer to choose a competitor. Even if you don't think of it being a competition, it very well is. The buyer has limited resources, you and plenty of other sellers want some of those resources, and there will be winners and losers.

Here are a few ideas that might get you started as you begin to identify where your point of difference arises:

- **The idea itself:** If your idea is, in fact, original, it may stand alone because, well, it is different. For instance, the Dyson vacuum cleaner was the first to use a cyclonic action to separate dust from air, meaning that you no longer required a bag or a filter, and no longer would the suction grow weaker the more you used it without emptying the bag. This truly was an innovation in home vacuum products. Now, everyone makes cyclonic vacuum cleaners, and Dyson relies on legacy brand associations and quality design as its point of difference.
- **X-factor:** Using quality design as Dyson now does is an example of looking for that X-factor to differentiate your offering. Or, your idea may be to start a coaching business. There are already other coaching businesses, but your point of difference lies in the personal quality you bring to the coaching experience through your personality. This is pretty hard to communicate, but it is a point of difference nonetheless.
- **Price:** You could always offer what you are selling for a cheaper price, assuming that price is a factor. You could work for less, do more for the same

76

price, and basically offer a better-value solution. The problem with this is that once you start on the discounting route, it is hard to get off, as your competitors may choose to do the same thing. However, to get a start and build some momentum it may actually be a good strategy. Just don't get locked into it. At some point you need to jack those low prices back up. On the flip side, you could differentiate yourself by being the most expensive. Buyers cannot help but wonder if perhaps you are more expensive because you are the best. I would go for this latter option every time. Countless experiments have linked price to a buyer's perceived value.

- **Quality:** Your solution, idea, product may be better. You will need evidence and features that support this notion, but it is a powerful point of difference if it is true. This is how management consultant Peter Fuda from The Alignment Partnership differentiates himself. He has PhD-supported research showing a success rate for transformation above 90 percent, when the average is closer to 30 percent. It is hard to argue with those numbers.

- **Speed:** In today's world, time is a premium currency. If you can save people time, solve their problems faster, this alone constitutes a competitive advantage. FedEx built an entire business on this promise.

- **Brand:** The personal identity that comes with being associated with you and your offer may be

77

attractive to the buyer. This is hard to do if you are on the left side of the mental barrier, because you probably do not have much of a reputation preceding your offer. However, as you will discover in the next competency of Influence, there are ways to do this, such as partnering with other brands. Harley-Davidson are attempting to stand out in the minds of young riders by being the primary sponsor of the Ultimate Fighting Championship.

- **You:** It will, in most cases, be impossible to separate yourself from your idea. And I can assure you, again as you will discover in the Influence competency, that many buyers will engage with the person as much, or even more so, than they will with the idea. Trusting and believing in you will be key in getting the buyer to engage. Barack Obama was elected as much for his personality and ability to inspire people as he was for the understanding that voters had about his policies. His background was also the natural target for his competitors to seek to exploit to negatively impact his ratings as President once he was there. As was his ability with words.

Finally, I need to sound a note of warning. There are ways of being credibly different and there are obtuse and distasteful ways of standing out. I believe it is key to know the difference. Very recently, I released a report to the media that was indirectly construed as me criticizing a section of the education community that I work very heavily

78

with. Some very high profile media slammed this group with one of my companies' names behind the news reports.

Now, there is a saying that any attention is good attention. I disagree entirely. I liken what happened in this instance to me insulting my friends in front of all of their friends and family, like the best man who delivers a speech with the one story you know he shouldn't tell.

And, perhaps less obvious and more nuanced is the fact that if you are personally so out of synch with your market that it rejects you on the premise of difference, you may have gone too far. In short, you may need a dose of common sense when looking for ways to stand out from the crowd. My advice is don't be cheap and tacky: it will make you seem cheap and tacky—which, as you will discover, is enough to get people to take notice and almost never enough to get them to buy.

79

ESTABLISHING A COMPELLING NEED

6

YOU ARE ALREADY on your way to discovering what makes your offer compelling. This chapter will give you a much better idea of what that really means and how you can pull it off. Remember, sharpness helps you pierce the attention barrier, and being compelling helps you pierce the intention barrier.

If you want to create real intention in the mind of buyers, you need to do one of two things:

1. Align your offer with a known market need: You convince buyers that you have a solution to a problem they know they have.
2. Move the market: You convince buyers that they have a problem they didn't know they had, and that you have a solution to that problem.

Consider this visual demonstration.

Being compelling

Your offer is the circle on the left. The market need (and there will be many) is the circle on the right. Compelling positioning is where you get those circles to overlap in the mind of the buyer. It is as simple, and as difficult, as that.

Let's start with developing a better understanding of what we mean by a market need and what this means for your idea.

EASY TO NEED

I am going to stick with the "easy to" concept here and elsewhere in the book. Mental energy is in short supply in the marketplace these days, and being "easy to," whether it is easy to understand, easy to differentiate or easy to need, and so on, will ensure that your offer does not consume a critical amount of the buyer's energy, causing him or her to reject it out of hand because considering it is simply too much effort.

To be easy to need, you have to align your offer with something the market wants/needs. Is what you're sell-

81

ing going to add value? If so, how will the buyer be able to measure that value? Is it going to meet a need? If so, what need does it meet? Are people looking for the solutions you offer? It is time you stopped reading for a moment to see if you can answer some of these very questions.

Breaking through the intention barrier has been a question at the heart of many decades of research. It has been studied, restudied and studied again. We are, after all, trying at this point to motivate people to buy. Based on all the research, one of the oldest explanations of what motivates buyers still serves us best. It is that human beings are driven by their desire to gain pleasure or to avoid pain. This notion goes back at least as far as the ancient Greeks and Epicureanism. It was the centerpiece of some of Freud's work, as well as some of the defining works of the 1960s, such as Victor Vroom's expectancy theory, which attempts to show the connection between action and reward. And, if you think about it, it is pretty obvious. We do things that give us more of what we want and less of what we don't.

If you want to align your offer to a market need, you will need to show how it either gives people more of what they want or helps them avoid what they don't want. This is what I call being "easy to need." In other words, you present your offer in such a way that it is obvious to the buyer how it can do one or both of the desired things.

One way to spin this theory in the context of positioning our offer is to align what we have with a need/want that the buyer is looking to satisfy. I have heard it said, "You need to identify the buyers' points of pain and show them how your proposition solves them."

There is good reason why people focus heavily on the pain aspects. It is generally understood that, in the moment of pain, humans will do more to avoid it than they would have done to prevent it. Now, that is not to say we are not motivated by the chance at a better future; we are—just not as strongly, perhaps, as the desire to alleviate an immediate problem. This is especially true because often the action required to avoid future pain requires some sort of short-term sacrifice. Exercising to stay healthy; eating well: both require giving up something pleasurable in the short term. Think about the last time you were sick. I bet that while you were sick you swore you would eat healthily when you got better. Did you? Exactly!

But don't beat yourself up; it's human nature. Did you know that studies have shown that 90 percent or more of people who have had invasive heart surgery never change their lifestyle habits after surgery even though it kills them?

It is as though our values flip. When we're sick to our stomachs, we want that pain to end. When we're feeling fine, we don't want to endure the short-term pain of giving up the immediately gratifying junk food. As the seller, you need to be aware of the buyer's immediate context, and how it is likely to change, so you can position your offer to fit within that context. Leading up to the global financial crisis, money was being made hand over fist by enabling people to get into more debt. In the midst of the credit crunch, equally large amounts of money were being made helping these very same customers to get out of debt. Same market, different need.

Perhaps a little paradoxically, but very powerful if you are selling professional services, is the fact that many buyers

83

don't know what their pain is, or what they need, but they know they have it. This is increasingly commonplace, and is the driving force behind the multi-billion dollar management consulting industry. The complexity of the current business landscape, the constant change we all face, the increasing workloads we have and pressure to do more with less, mean big companies often miss the forest because they are so deep in the trees.

Consultants perform the extremely valuable—despite the jokes, companies would have stopped paying long ago if there was no value—function of shedding light on their challenges, and hopefully a road map for turning them around. The need you solve in this case is identifying the need itself.

Let me give you an example of positioning an offer as a solution to a point of pain that the market has, but to shake it up let's use an internal example. Say you are an employee in the pharmaceutical industry and you are in the research-and-development (R&D) team. You have a vision of being a player on the multinational stage. Your idea is to do so in the R&D space. You have two choices. The first is to put your head down, work hard and basically do what you are told and wait for those opportunities to be presented to you. The second is to be proactive and go out of your way to position yourself as the company's solution to a major problem it faces. I like the second option, don't you?

Here is what you might do. By being a student of the industry and listening at all the off-sites you are made to attend, you realize that one of the major challenges facing the organization is that the days of the massive, global mega-drug are over. A combination of transparency leading to increased competition, changes to drug administration

84

and patents, and the fact that medicine is moving towards more targeted and personalized treatments is changing the very business model of your company.

You know this threatens the profitability of the whole industry and that it is most likely the issue that keeps your senior leaders up at night, including the ones you will need to influence if you are to become a player on the multinational stage. Instead of just confining yourself to your cubicle and doing good work, you decide to become the resident expert on changing pharmaceutical business models, and while there is no way you can understand all the science, you begin to understand deeply the role R&D plays in the future success of the company.

You interview in-house scientists, read journal articles and talk to industry experts about what organizations will need to do to respond to these changes. What you learn is that the speed with which an idea can be brought through its R&D processes to become a product will ultimately be what differentiates one organization from the next in your highly competitive industry. This new insight allows you to further sharpen your idea from being an expert in the broad-ranging field of pharmaceutical R&D to becoming a specialist in speeding up the R&D process itself.

So now you start to study how to speed up the R&D process. You learn that a chemical-products company of similar scale to yours has achieved this in its industry, halving its R&D time by outsourcing key functions to world-wide networks of highly specialized academics and budding PhD students. (For a real-life example, check out NineSigma developed by P&G and Innocentive, a spin-off company of pharma giant Eli Lilly.)

You run a trial of this new form of R&D in your small, focused area of research and get a breakthrough in a third less time. You write a paper about it and suggest you present it at the next regional meeting for heads of R&D, chaired by none other than the big kahuna you have been trying to get in front of. Actually, if you were really smart you would realize that your direct boss is also part of your market, so you would suggest the two of you co-present the findings so he gets some of the kudos his ego desires too, thus preventing any attempt he might make to sabotage you.

If you are still fearful of him stealing your idea, you could write and publish the paper before suggesting the partnership to him. That way, it has your name all over it. You even suggest sending this information to the attendees prior to the meeting you intend to co-present it at.

You do the presentation, which you worked on for days, and it rocks. You have the data, the examples and plenty of supporting evidence to back up your findings on the future of R&D, and as a result the global head decides you should head up a new project trialing this model, only this time at a much larger scale. You are the obvious choice because no one else has done the research.

The sharpness of your specialty and the relevance to the industry at the time gets you on the mental menu of the big decision-makers much faster than if you had stayed general, kept your head down and worked your way up the ranks. In a way, your proactive work has created a whole new position.

Most importantly, though, you have perfectly positioned yourself and your expertise as the solution to a problem the business knows it has and that it has been trying to remedy for some time. Who knows? You may in time decide that there is a consultancy business in this and leave your corporate post to help other pharmaceutical companies with the problem.

This is an example of aligning yourself to a recognized market need. In this case, it goes one step further and pioneers a new solution, and it is exactly what makes you the go-to person. And this is what great positioning does—it sets up you and your idea as a solution to a problem the market knows it has.

Again, Salesforce.com nailed this strategy when it built the entire mission of its business on the desire to end software. There is no shortage of companies and decision makers frustrated by the limitations of the existing model of software. Things like:

- Expensive license fees.
- The need to have it on every system/machine.
- The multiple devices data is stored on.
- The complexity of data synchronization.
- The headache of upgrades.
- The business models of All or Nothing when it comes to upgrades.

And on the list could go. This is clearly a pain-point. The potency of the Salesforce.com model however, is not that it had indentified a pain-point that its offer could solve, but that it moved an entire market towards the concept of Software as a Service and enterprise grade cloud-computing. We will look at this in more detail in

87

just a moment; for now, though, let's dissect the Pharmaceutical R&D model to identify its replicable elements.

- **Being proactive:** First and foremost, you were proactive and did not wait for the opportunity to present itself or the market need to find you.
- **Basing your action on research:** The decision of what area to focus on was made after doing some research, talking to people in the know and making a personal judgement about where your industry was headed.
- **Timing it right:** Your judgement proved correct, as not only your industry but also others were looking for a new way of doing R&D. In effect, you were on trend.
- **Displaying proof:** You had proof. By conducting a small, under-the-radar trial, you were able to show you had a theoretical understanding of the potential of this new model but more importantly that it could be proven to deliver significantly improved outcomes.
- **Staying targeted:** You did not try to make yourself famous. You did not try to present at the global executive meeting. You presented to the heads of R&D, who ultimately would be responsible for your immediate progress.
- **Playing the game:** You did not go over your boss's head, instead bringing him along for the ride and allowing him to receive some credit too.

88

All of this talk reminds me of when I was first starting my business speaking in schools. Unlike the example above, what I am about to share with you did not take the many months that would be needed to position yourself as an expert in R&D through research and trials. What I am about to tell you is how I revolutionized my business by changing a few words in the headline of my marketing materials. A process that merely took minutes, after of course testing my offer in the market.

It was in my early days and I had just read the iconic book *Tested Advertising Methods* by the direct-mail guru John Caples. It recommended trialing different headlines when marketing your idea. Here are the ones I tried:

"Informative seminars for school students."
"Career and study program for students."
"Short, inspiring seminars for teenagers."
"Do your students need motivating?"

Which one do you think got the greatest response?

The last one was more than twice as effective at generating a response than the other three. Now, the interesting thing is, the other three were much more indicative of what I was trying to sell, but they did not appeal enough to the need that the actual buyers of my seminars had. What teacher doesn't think their students need motivating?

At this point, you may be feeling as though what you are selling really isn't about a problem. Maybe all those seminars you have been to have blessed you with a permanent positive attitude. What you sell is about possibility.

89

Well, let me just say this. Selling seminars to schools was, in my mind, about potential. It was about helping a generation of teenagers seize the opportunities that lay before them. However, if you really think about it, even such a "positive" offer suggests there is a problem with the students. This is just another way of saying that I had a solution to the problem of unfulfilled potential, and offering someone more of what they want is just another way of saying they currently haven't got enough.

One of the great challenges of the human condition is that enough is never enough. It is as if we can never have enough money, or a fast enough car or a big enough house. You might argue here that you are not that materialistic, in which case let me say it this way: you can never have enough fulfillment, enough love, enough family time, or enough spiritual connection. I am going to unpack this in much more detail a little later, but if you are interested the field of evolutionary psychology offers great insight into why enough is never enough. Check out Dr P. R. Lawrence, a professor of organizational behavior at Harvard, for some great writing on this topic. My point here is that in order to get others engaged in your pursuit of more, your best chance lies in finding out what they want more of and then offering them a solution to this "problem."

So take out a pen and start answering the following questions:

- What problem does my offer solve?
- What does my offer help the buyer avoid?
- What does it help the buyer get more of?
- How can I best make that clear?

- How can I go about proving my solution does that?
- How is my solution different from all the other solutions in the market already?

EASY TO SUPPORT

It is generally agreed that products have life cycles. Below is a rough diagram of what the average cycle looks like. The type of product, the market and therefore how quickly it rises in popularity determine the shape of the curve.

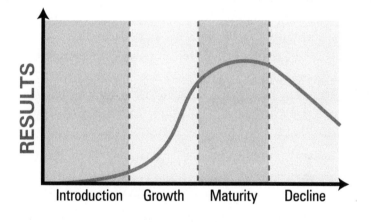

Life cycle of an offer

Now, although the diagram generally refers to specific products, the concept applies to much larger movements too. I believe a key to being compelling is to try to stay on trend. Before you assume that a trend is something that comes and goes, and that you will need to constantly rein-

91

vent yourself, I want you to realize that some trends can last many decades. The power of being on trend is that you will be able to position yourself as relevant in the mind of the buyer because the problem for which you have a solution will already be on the buyer's mind.

Let's consider the profession of accounting as an example. While accountants are not going anywhere soon, there is no question that certain specialties and even fads occur within the industry. Trusts have been a boon for the accounting industry for many years now, but crackdowns by respective tax authorities have made them less attractive for tax planning in recent years. Offshore activity was the same, and it is now subject to more scrutiny than ever before. Primary-industry investments in things such as pine plantations, abalone farms and other eclectic assets with tax benefits have proved popular with the wealthy Baby Boomer generation.

My point is, aligning your idea or your new business with a trend or shift in perceived needs is a big win when it comes to being compelling. Even if your offering is in an age-old profession such as accounting, there will still be trends within the industry, and you should align yourself to those trends. The early you get on it, the better. Think about it this way: many existing accounting practices will be rooted in doing business the way they have always done business. Generally speaking, they will be slower to adjust to emerging trends than your brand-new and highly nimble practice.

If you solve a problem, then you are easy to need. If you solve a problem that is right in the sweet spot for the business, then it is much easier to support the decision to

92

engage you. Think about it carefully. Every buyer that you are trying to sell to is also trying to sell to someone else, be it his or her boss, partner or the board. He or she will need to be able to support the decision to engage you, and being on trend makes this much easier to do. If everyone is talking about this new approach to accounting, it is much more likely that the buyer's buyers will know about it.

Or, put differently, no one pulls all the strings. Everyone has to answer to someone, and being on trend makes it easier for the buyer to justify the decision to engage you. If the whole world is talking about environmental sustainability, a CEO will find it easier to justify his decision to invest in biodiesel delivery trucks (as Tesco in the UK did) to the analysts and shareholders. If leadership is a buzzword in business circles, it will be easier to sell your workshops if they can be under the guise of "leadership development," rather than say "management training."

Every buyer that you are trying to sell to is also trying to sell to someone else, be it his or her boss, partner, or the board.

It breaks my heart to share this with you but a good friend of mine, after many years of working for someone else, finally decided to go out and do his own thing. It was 2008, which as we all know was not the greatest year for business around the world. But wait for it. His idea was to build a mentoring network for hedge-fund managers. Great idea, but in the year he started it, more than half the hedge funds he was targeting did not make it to the end of the year. Huge losses on the market, bans on short-selling and frozen credit mar-

93

kets all but destroyed much of the industry. Great idea, off trend.

Now, had he been in the business of restructuring hedge funds to free up capital, he would most certainly have been on trend. As the diagram above indicated, things have a cycle. They start slow, gather momentum and eventually mature and die off. Focus on what need is growing in importance and how your proposition can meet it, rather than focusing on a need that is mature, likely well serviced already and potentially going to die off soon.

No one pulls all the strings.

I want to return now to my example of, "Do your students need motivating?" If you take this one step further, you can get even sharper when it comes to the pain points you solve. To flesh out my offer, I created a grid with the three grades of students I was targeting on the horizontal and eight half-terms down the vertical. What this allowed me to do was to become very focused on which pain points would be the most pertinent at certain times of the year, so I could convince the teachers to pay me to come and speak to their students about the right thing at the right time. When exam time was near, "stress management" was big. When the school year was just starting, "getting motivated" was the thrust of my offer. The more targeted I got the easier it was for me to be easy to support. What principal could say no to a teacher requesting a small amount of funding to help their senior students manage the mounting stress as they approached their final examinations? In other words, my table and the language

94

I used helped my buyer to support his or her decision in front of his or her buyer.

Having said that, I have screwed this up as often as I have got it right. Much more recently, I have been faced with a major case of mistiming that thankfully may be righting itself as we speak. Getting your timing right can be just as important as getting your offer right. If you are like me, your aspirations expand beyond making more money or getting famous. One of my goals in life is to change the lifestyle habits of the next generation. Diabetes and obesity are off the charts, and binge drinking is seen by many as out of control.

Now, I don't just talk about it. I started, and remain, the CEO of a very successful consultancy that undertakes large-scale behavioral change projects. This was my reinvention (see Competency 5). My consultancy is called ChangeLabs, and it works with more than 500,000 people every year, in more than 10,000 sessions in multiple countries. We deliver a massive financial literacy program, teaching teenagers how to take control of their financial future. We work in hundreds of schools every year on integrating technology into teachers' classrooms in pedagogically sound ways, and we run groundbreaking workshops for corporations to drive collaboration in the workplace and hopefully increase national productivity.

For years, we have been trying to get a program up in Australia on the topic of binge drinking. It is not that we are opposed to drinking—I personally love a beer or two with friends—it is the culture of getting smashed for the sake of it that is obviously unhealthy. Having seen it firsthand as a

95

former bar manager, I know the damage this habitual behavior can do to people's lives and relationships.

Now, I pride myself on being able to make things happen but for the life of me I have not been able to crack this nut. I have failed time and time again to get this program funded. It seemed as though no one was listening. Then a new prime minister was elected and one of the big things he was talking about was binge drinking among young adults and teenagers. Without getting into it, a series of new taxes were introduced and funding distributed and all of a sudden there were research groups with the ability to fund one of our change initiatives.

It was now time to get noticed. If someone was looking for people with new and innovative approaches to education and behavioral change, our track record suggested we were the best game in town. I can't tell you whether or not we will pull it off—I am still in negotiations at the time of writing—but I can tell you that all of a sudden people were returning my calls. Timing has made all the difference between getting on the mental menu in this area and not. We had changed nothing in regard to the idea; all that changed was the timing and with it a zeitgeist shift that made it easy to support funding a program on binge drinking. If the Prime Minister thinks it is a good idea and is funding research and action in this area, that is pretty easy to support, wouldn't you say?

The same is happening in the area of obesity in the U.S. At present, Michelle Obama has launched a national campaign on healthy eating for kids. As world leaders in behavior change, this is an obvious area of interest for my company, but it has become much easier to get access to funds since this became a national movement, with significant government funding. In this case there is no need to move the market, it is moving all by itself.

The interesting thing about trends such as this, is that they all look obvious in hindsight. Or at least the businesses that rode on the back of them do. Let me give you a recent example of this to make the point.

I travel a lot in my work, to the extent that in recent years I have made the U.S. my base. At first, I lived in Los Angeles, and while I was there the Urth Caffé was the place to be seen in. It is where Vinnie Chase and the boys hang out on the television show *Entourage*. And in real life it is where the models and actors go for their coffee. Personally, I did not think its coffee was very good, but the cafe had a powerful story and was on a powerful trend.

If you visit its website, Urth claims to have five strict standards for selecting its coffee. Here is its fourth: "Source farms must pay their coffee workers a fair wage in order to improve the workers' quality of life. Urth Caffé representatives or reputable organizations must be invited to check the claims of fair wages by visiting workers' villages."

These days, this practice is known as Fair Trade, but Urth Caffé had been following these principles for some years before it was the "in thing" to do. Today, everyone seems to be claiming they buy only produce that has been grown without exploiting the communities that grow it.

It seems obvious now that this would be a powerful marketing ploy for a coffee seller, especially when you consider the kind of buyer who spends $4 on a cup of coffee. What Urth achieved by getting on this trend early is firstly a point of difference and secondly a justification for why it was charging so much for its coffee. In this case, the buyer's "other buyer" was his or her own conscience. We will explore this individual process of support when we talk about being "easy to justify" under the Influence competency.

The key to being easy to support is to make sure the market need to which you are attempting to appeal is identifiable and convincing enough for the buyer to easily demonstrate to his or her own boss.

So the question to answer now is how do you identify a trend?

- Use online trend polls that are based on what people are searching and sharing. Here are a few to check out:
  - www.google.com/trends
  - www.trendpedia.com
  - www.facebook.com/advertising/?lexicon
  - www.blogpulse.com
  - www.trendrr.com
  - http://adlab.msn.com/
- Subscribe to different websites and newsletters. Your job is not to become an expert in spotting trends—unless, of course, that is your offer. There are already plenty of people doing this. Here are some sites I recommend:
  - www.trendwatching.com
  - www.trendhunter.com
  - www.pewresearch.org

- www.harrisinteractive.com
- www.technorati.com
- The list could go on and on, but it would not be a bad idea to subscribe to these for starters.

■ Ask lots of questions and listen. Seriously, it is not that hard. If you are paying close attention to what is on the agenda of company conferences and team meetings in your target market, you will get a pretty good idea pretty quickly of what is on this market's mind. You could also go one step further and ask. When I was launching *Generation Y*, I asked a few executives what the biggest challenge in relation to the new generation would be and they came back with the same issue: retention. Now I knew that investing in staff retention was going to be a hot trend.

■ Be on the lookout for trends. It sounds ridiculous, I know, but just being aware that you are looking out for emerging trends makes you more likely to find them. The more specific you are in defining what you are trying to do—such as searching for emerging trends—and the more time you spend making this a reality, the more likely your brain will be to pay attention and find things that will improve your ability to pull it off. Call this luck if you like, but the people who spot new trends are generally those who are already immersed in the area and looking for them. I call it hard work.

Ask yourself the following questions:

99

- What trends currently exist in the area of your offering that you could "pin" your idea to?
- What trends exist outside of the market you serve that could be introduced into your market (think Urth and Fair Trade) to make your offer even more compelling?
- What are buyers being asked to find solutions for by their buyers (bosses, clients, investors) and how could your offer be seen as a possible solution?

Now, any conversation about identifying trends involves some risk. And inevitably our own fear about backing the wrong trend arises. Think back to the pharmaceutical R&D example we used under the heading "Easy to Need." The problem with this example is that I assumed I was right about the trend towards outsourcing the R&D function in the pharmaceuticals industry. What if I am wrong?

I am not in R&D in pharmaceuticals. I could be wrong, and so could you. That is no excuse not to try. Players make bets. Your success in making it happen requires that you take risks. Do your research, sure, but at some point you need to make some bets.

MOVING
THE MARKET

THERE IS ONE alternative to identifying and following a trend, of course (which is certainly not without its risks), and that is to get the ball rolling yourself. What if, after all your packaging, all your research and all your trend seeking, you realize that there is no recognized market need? Yet you are certain that what you are offering has legs and that a massive trend is on its way—you are just coming in before it has got started?

Then you move the market! Just saying that gets me juiced. The thought of being so committed and so excited by your idea that you would persist in spite of the fact that no one seems to care is both admirable and insane at the same time. I have no problem with the crazy part though. In a way, you have to be a little crazy to make big things happen.

And, truth be told, if your idea is original enough, you will likely find yourself needing to move the market, because you will be selling something no one knows they need. You should see this as both exciting and challenging at the same time. If you think it is hard to align yourself with an existing problem, try convincing the buyers that they have yet another problem they need to solve.

This is exactly what Salesforce.com did with Software as a Service and cloud computing. In 1999 when Mark Benioff started Salesforce.com, the concept of the web browser being the operating system and accessing software that was hosted and managed on the internet instead of your computer, and the business model of monthly access fees for such a service was a very new idea in the technology industry.

Their early success grew the credibility of both the business model and the mode of accessing data online, and as you would expect spurred a number of competitors to aggressively enter the space. Rather than negatively impact Salesforce.com's growth, it accelerated it instead. Major CRM providers like Siebel launched their cloud CRM offerings, and were able to further move the market based on their size, significant sales teams and the credibility such a respected provider gives to an emerging technology.

The good thing for Salesforce.com is that due to their willingness to stay focused earlier their growth, they genuinely did have a superior offer which allowed them to go head to head with industry giants and win. If you think about it, if the market moves, as the online CRM market had, then any serious buyer will look at all credible alternative vendors, and Salesforce.com was one of them.

Their name is virtually synonymous with Online CRM and cloud-computing.

I thought it would be useful now to outline some strategies companies have used successfully to move the market. The truth is, there is no one way to move a market. I have no doubt that, to do it effectively, you will need to follow more than one of the examples given here, and you will need the media on your side, some lucky breaks and a bucket-load of persistence.

OFFER IT

I did not know I needed a big, flat-screen TV until I saw it. And when I did, I knew immediately that my life would never be complete until I had one. I absolutely had to have one. Now, I wasn't prepared to pay the $10,000 price tag for a 40-inch model that frankly did not look that great anyway and weighed as much as a small car, but I did know I would certainly buy one when they became competitive. The popularity of these TVs is phenomenal, and it is no coincidence that the explosion in sales occurred side by side with an explosion in consumer credit around the world. This really was a case of build it and they will come. Just making the newer, better model available in the category moved the market. Now, it seems, I and the rest of America need a 3D television—thanks, *Avatar*—a film which single handedly moved the market and spurred an onslaught of 3D Hollywood releases.

There is a pretty good chance, however, that your idea and your market power are such that it won't be a case of

103

build it and they will come. There is every chance that your idea, like so many others, will be ignored and rejected before it is widely embraced and accepted. To move the market this easily, you need a lot of influence, and a lot of market power. Pioneer and the other early purveyors of big-screen plasma and LCD TVs had a global distribution channel and a very well respected brand.

FORCE IT

There is no question that the big music labels did not want to embrace iTunes in the way Apple wanted them to. But it came down to a matter of either embracing iTunes and other digital distribution platforms or letting people keep stealing music on the web.

When you look at Apple's virtual domination of the digital-music-player market and the ease of using the iTunes program itself, you start to see the power the company has in its negotiations with the music labels. No one knows for sure the exact ins and outs of every label deal with Apple, but the New York Times estimates that the wholesale cost of a song for Apple is potentially as high as $0.80. When you consider that much of the infrastructure is a fixed cost (there are no additional warehousing and distribution costs after bandwidth) and you start doing the numbers in billions, you can see this is a very profitable business indeed. The more ubiquitous iPods and iTunes become, the more Apple will be able to "force" the market to embrace its platform—the market in this case being the labels, rather than the end users.

Apple of course has replicated their ability to drive certain platforms with the success of the iPhone and more recently the iPad. The explosion of such devices onto the market has meant that many of the best apps are on the Apple platform. Anyone looking to distribute content will want to be available on the Apple iTunes network, based purely on Apple's market power. Interestingly though, Apple did attempt to force the market away from Flash but eventually had to cave to market pressure as too many sites used Flash technology to display images and video that Apple needed to oblige.

This would not be a successful strategy in most cases because there aren't that many people with that much power over the market. But that is not to say it can't happen. Think of how many more "home" brands are appearing on the shelves of supermarkets, at the expense of the major brands, in an attempt to force the customers to choose the brands of the store itself. Less shelf space in supermarkets is the same as saying fewer sales. And when you add to this that these very same supermarkets who sell their home brand force the large food companies to produce the product for them under threat that if they don't they will stop stocking their products across the board you realize that, at the big end of town, force is a legitimate strategy. Depending on your market position, you may even be able to employ it yourself.

The mere mortals among us, though, are likely to need to be a little more covert. We should probably consider the practice of seeding it.

SEED IT

A man from India once wrote, "In America is the place, the people, the opportunity for everything new." That man's name was Swami Vivekananda, and he is generally seen as the pioneer of the Western yoga movement. The popularity of yoga, or at least its mainstream acceptance, seems to be a recent phenomenon. If someone had told me that Swami had first visited America in the early 1960s, I would have no hesitation in believing it. As it turns out, he said those words in 1893!

Yoga has long been a grass-roots movement. It was in the 1920s that Paramahansa Yogananda wrote his rather modernly titled book *Recharge Your Business Batteries Out of the Cosmos*, using yoga and the beliefs that underpin it as his foundation. By 1950, the first "clinic" had opened in Hollywood, followed closely by another in San Francisco. By 1961, yoga had made its way to the TV screen and now it is a $3-billion-plus business with more than 15 million participants. And that is just in the U.S.

You could argue that its recent meteoric rise is due to the imbalance we all feel between work and life, and the added stress that 24/7 connectivity brings, but in reality the idea of Westerners seeking enlightenment from Eastern practices was seeded many years before we had BlackBerrys.

The good news for you is that you won't have to wait more than a century for your idea to become a reality. If you seed it properly, it can literally explode overnight. Firstly, because the cost of distribution and your ability to publish is virtually zero with the internet, and if the crowd, likes what you offer, it can spread rapidly. Or you could use a bit of product placement too.

In April 2009, Hugo Chávez, president of Venezuela, handed President Barack Obama a 35-year-old book called *Open Veins of Latin America*, by Eduardo Galeano. The day before, its Amazon sales rank was 54,000. A few days after, it was the second-highest-selling book on Amazon. It dropped back down the charts just as quickly, mind you.

So how can you use this? Well, my eldest sister, Mez, is a bit of a serial entrepreneur. Among other things, she has started a very successful little fashion label called Muu Muus by Mez. She buys stunning silk fabrics from China and has them made into various different summer "throw overs" for women. They have been a huge hit in the well-to-do eastern suburbs of Sydney. Anyway, Grace Jones bought one and a picture of her wearing one was featured in the social pages, and the rest is history, as they say.

Now, I know the next question is how did she get Grace Jones to buy one? She didn't. But she did deliberately set up at a market on Bondi Beach in Australia, famous for its celebrity visitors and residents, and therefore the clicking cameras of trashy magazines. She could have set up in any one of a dozen other markets but the Bondi location was a deliberate choice in that it is famous for being a celebrity hangout.

Ask yourself, how can you seed your idea in a way that will have it spread? Better still, how can you spread it to people with influence?

107

NAME IT

Have you ever watched television late at night? I swear, within two hours you will be convinced that you have at least three illnesses or syndromes that you were not previously even aware of:

Are you human?

Do you lie in bed at night?

Are your legs sometimes restless?

Then you have Restless Leg Syndrome.

Talk to your doctor immediately about prescribing you Leglesscyllin.

And then, in rapid, almost incomprehensible, speech: "Leglesscyllin has some side effects that include brain tumors, erectile dysfunction, and death. If you have any of these symptoms, please see your doctor."

Then back to the normal speech: "Leglesscyllin will put an end to the unhappiness that has plagued your life because of Restless Leg Syndrome. Live the life you were meant to live, today. Leglesscyllin, for a good night's sleep."

Now, this is a deliberately silly example, but the point is that finding a problem or situation and naming it works to generate interest. Tim O'Reilly named the new social media phenomenon Web 2.0 as far back as 2004 when he used this label for his annual-conference theme. Now he is synonymous with the idea and his conferences are among the most in demand in this field on earth.

As the competition for smart people intensified in the mid-1990s, McKinsey & Co. released a paper terming it a "War for Talent." This became the catch cry of many HR professionals the world over, and well into the new millennium the term was still being used by anyone selling a solution related to human resources. Their services would be presented as "your key to winning the war for talent." McKinsey became strongly associated with the war for talent and, by extension, with insightful and progressive thinking in general.

BRAND IT

If naming it is about labeling the problem, branding it is about labeling its solution.

After the Second World War, Japanese manufacturers started eating the American manufacturers for lunch. Or at least their market share. The Japanese managed to turn their image around as the makers of cheap and poor-quality equipment to being the world's leading producer of cars and consumer electronics.

The Americans, for the most part, were unable to understand why or how this happened. Or who was behind it. No doubt, a revealing documentary in 1980 on NBC titled *If Japan Can . . . Why Can't We?* shocked a few U.S. executives when they learned that the techniques they were using were based on principles developed way back in the 1920s by Walter Shewhart at Bell Telephone Laboratories and that the man behind the turnaround, including the loss of American competitiveness, was an American named William Edwards Deming.

What I love about Deming's story and the frenzy that followed the adoption of his methodology after the airing of the documentary is the cool term that he used to brand

109

his ideas. Shewhart had called the process Statistical Process Control. Boring! Deming called it Kaizen, which is a Japanese word meaning constant improvement.

Not to be outdone, other American management consultants have borrowed from the work of Shewhart and Deming and come up with their own brands. These include Quality Management, Total Quality Management (branded TQM, of course), Business Process Improvement and, my favorite, Six Sigma.

Since being implemented and branded by Bill Smith of Motorola in 1986, Six Sigma has gone on to become a religion in some organizations. A massive industry has been spawned, with trainers and consultants who are certified and receive "belts" in the same way one would in karate. The most in demand are called Black Belts, and internally this is seen as an honor in many Six Sigma companies.

I have no interest here in debating the role of Six Sigma in a company's competitiveness and ability to innovate, only to say you cannot deny the power it has exerted on the companies that have embraced it. It is amazing what branding can do.

Ask yourself, how can you brand your solution? Jot down some cool titles that could become the brand for your idea.

And this is not just useful for intellectual-property-based businesses. Consider the Les Mills gym franchise. Olympian Les Mills started the company in New Zealand many years ago, before his son, Phillip, took it over and dramatically expanded it into the global success it is today.

In 1980, Phillip developed an aerobic workout program to music for his New Zealand Les Mills gyms that

110

became all the rage in fitness circles. As a result, he developed a few more and started licensing across the Tasman to gyms in Australia. Before long, he had developed a whole series of programs, which included:

- BodyPump—done with weights.
- RPM—done on a stationary bicycle.
- BodyStep—floor aerobics.
- BodyCombat—floor aerobics.
- BodyJam—floor aerobics.
- BodyAttack—floor aerobics.

These days, it is estimated that more than four million people around the world participate in a Les Mills program of some description, in 55 countries and more than 10,000 gyms. Not bad for a kid from Auckland.

The best thing about a branded package is you can communicate it clearly, spin a whole lot of issues as relating to it, and then spread this packaged solution as the next must-have in the market you serve.

SPREAD IT

The truth is, once you have seeded your idea and branded it, you want to build some buzz around the new need you are trying to convince people they have. Nothing spreads faster than a good story. Develop some highly emotive stories that relate to this new market need and use the media, and social media, to spread them.

111

One person who did this very well is Sean Belnick, whom I interviewed a few years ago for Fox Business. Sean started an online office-furniture retailer called Biz-chair.com in 2001 with the help of his stepfather, Gary Glazer, who was a veteran of the furniture business. Using Sean's coding and web prowess and Gary's understanding of the industry, they launched their site. A combination of good search rankings and great publicity helped grow this little internet start-up to the $50-million-per-year retailer it is today. The question is, why did Bizchair.com get so much publicity? Because Sean was only 14 years old. The teen entrepreneur is always a great story, and the media were quick to spread it.

You could try starting a blog, or creating a podcast, or maybe Twitter is your thing. Now, don't be fooled. There is no such thing as "blog it and they will come." There is as much rubbish and noise in the blogosphere these days as there is anywhere else. I would put it to you that it is probably just as difficult to get noticed and heard in the blogosphere as it is through traditional media. If anything, it may be easier in traditional media.

Local newspapers are starving for good ad revenue at the moment, and as such they have less staff than ever before. They are crying out for good local content, and I would sooner start here than I would in the blogosphere. You could, however, go crazy with YouTube and other video sites. The point is that you need to create some buzz around the new need.

112

No one I know of has done that better than Tom Dickson, the founder of Blendtec. How would you like more than 30 million people to have watched you promote how awesome your product is, for the cost of making a few home videos? Well, that is what Tom has managed to do with a few simple YouTube clips.

In late 2006, a video of the Blendtec Total Blender appeared on YouTube with some really cheesy old guy—an '80s TV commercial throwback—showing you how strong his blender is by blending golf balls. People thought it was funny and passed it on. Before you knew it, thousands of people had watched it, so he did another one. This time, though, he blended marbles.

Now, there is no way that everyone who watched this video did so because they wanted to buy a blender. No, they did so because they thought it was funny or cool to watch this goofy guy, who turned out to be Tom himself, blend some crazy shit. However, in the process Tom seeds the idea that their existing blender is not up to par and that they really need a much more powerful model. This is not a need they knew they had, but one that is at least subliminally planted after watching the video.

Tom now has a following, so he starts playing to the crowd. He blends the guitar from the Guitar Hero game because it has no Beach Boys on it. He blends the iPhone, getting more than six million hits from viewers. He even blends a whole lot of props designed to represent the U.S. stimulus package, and a camcorder, so you can watch from the camera's perspective what it would be like to get blended.

Tom has since launched a YouTube channel, and in addition to his tens of millions of viewers to date, there are

113

literally more than 200,000 people signed up to get his next installment. Perhaps the funniest thing of all is there are now "Will it Blend?" and "Tom Dickson is my Homeboy" T-shirts being sold. It has become a phenomenon.

Now, has it sold some blenders? Of course it has. Dickson won't say how many, but the fact that he keeps making these videos is a pretty good indication that he is doing just fine.

My point is this: there is no way in the space of a few years he would have managed to get word-of-mouth audiences and mentions in the tens of millions from selling blenders if he hadn't leveraged the phenomenal tools that the internet provides.

He literally moved the blender market. For some other amazing examples of the powerful role video can play spreading ideas please check out Gary Vaynerchuk who grew his family wine business from $4m to $60m in 5 years with a YouTube series on wine which was low-grade, simple, for the masses, and just plain interesting. Consider too Salman Khan and his Khan Academy which has created thousands of video tutorials for students the world over. All of which were filmed in a tiny section of his apartment, and through a simple web video set up. At the time of writing there were already 22 million views of his videos, and growing at 70,000 per day. Now that is Making It Happen—Khan is being held up as a model for the future of global education, and the likes of Bill Gates are reaching out to accelerate his impact.

UNCOVER IT

From time to time, someone seems to uncover something in a powerful way. The most obvious example in recent history is Al Gore and his film *An Inconvenient Truth*. If the truth be told, what Al Gore presented in his movie had in fact been published before. There was a very similar film made almost 50 years previously about the very same issues. But no one can deny the power of that more recent film and the way it has helped put the environment front and center on the agendas of people all over the world. Not only has Al Gore really had his idea embraced, he has become quite wealthy in the process. A win–win, I say.

I find it interesting to know that he spent eight years as the vice president and was far more able to progress the environmental agenda in one movie out of office than he could while he was in office. Either way, "uncovering" a new issue allows you to not only move the market but also, by default, position yourself as the expert on any and all related issues.

Are you able to expose, or uncover, something your market will be interested in hearing about? Have you discovered that your competitors have been lying to your future customers about their products? Have you discovered a groundbreaking perspective that helps define a currently unidentified problem?

This may seem very similar to "name it," but there is a difference. "Uncovering" involves the revelation of a conspiracy or a problem that everyone secretly knew was an issue but had been trying to deny. Exposing a dodgy political deal; exposing predatory tactics from major retailers; exposing the destruction of our natural environment: these are all examples of confronting the public with things they knew were going on but preferred to ignore.

EVENT IT

I was at a conference recently where they turned off the lights during the gala dinner, lighting the room almost entirely with candles to participate in Earth Hour. If you don't know Earth Hour, it is an annual event in which we are encouraged to extinguish all the lights in our home in an attempt to relieve some of the pressure on the world's resources. It is both a symbolic event to raise awareness and effective in that it really does reduce demand on the power grid in a significant way, albeit only for an hour.

Conceived in 2007 by the World Wildlife Fund in partnership with the Sydney Morning Herald, Earth Hour attracted more than two million Sydney participants on its first evening. Obviously, it was helped by the partnership with Australia's longest-running newspaper, but I can assure you that if it had not been made into an "event," it would never have been as effective.

So powerful was this first event that the following year more than 400 cities participated, and in 2010, its fourth year, more than 126 countries got involved. Phenomenal! Google even got in on the act, running a black home page with the line, "We have turned out the lights. Now it's your turn."

What sort of event can you build around your new idea, or the issue you are aiming to address? Remember, we are trying here to move the market and convince it that it needs what you are offering.

As a final thought, think back to the 30- and 40-hour famines from early in the book and the previously discussed music event where the price of entry was donating blood. These philanthropic causes are perfect examples of convincing people about the existence of issues they may not fully be aware of and then convincing them that they need to help do something about them. Events work.

I feel as though I have made "moving the market" sound like a sexy idea. It is! It is also bloody hard work. The landscape is littered with people, ideas and businesses that were convinced the market needed what they had to sell, and yet they were unable to make their mark. At some point, you do need to objectively question if your offer, your idea, your solution is a good one. And when you do this, you need to be humble enough to admit it if it is not. Seriously, there is such a thing as a bad idea. Even after all your packaging, after all your trend and market research, it may just turn out that people do not want what you have.

A humorous example I came across was inflatable underpants. In the same way that your car has airbags that inflate, someone developed a pair of underpants that would puff up when they sensed you were falling rapidly to the ground. I could be wrong, but I think this really is a dumb idea. Interesting (cute), sure, but really who would wear them? Maybe, just maybe, if the developer targeted his offer enough, he could appeal to a market of

117

older folk who were prone to falls and for whom a broken hip would be a real setback.

Let's assume, though, that your idea is not that bad and there really could be a market for it. You need to understand that any new idea will go through what is often referred to as an acceptance cycle. Your job is to hold your nerve as everyone around you seems to be fighting against your offer. Allow me to explain.

HOLDING YOUR NERVE

One of my favorite cities in the world is Verona, Italy. Not a large city, but a pretty one. It is where Shakespeare's *Romeo and Juliet* is set. In the heart of the old part of town is the piazza and the balcony from which Juliet utters those famous words, "O Romeo, Romeo, wherefore art thou Romeo?"

When I visited this piazza, there must have been at least 15 couples crammed into a small space engaging in one of two activities that would be deemed unacceptable anywhere else. Now, before you freak out, thinking I am going to write something totally inappropriate, it is not what you think. The first thing is scratching the initials of you and your lover with a "4" in between on the old brick walls of the apartments that encompass the piazza, and the other is having your photo taken with your hand caressing the right breast of a bronze statue of Juliet. Of course, in any other context the writing on the wall would be deemed graffiti, and as for rubbing a statue's breast, well, the last time I recall that being cool was when I was 14 and on a school field trip.

118

I wonder how many times people did either of these things and were scolded or frowned upon, even arrested, for disrespecting a very beautiful piazza before it became not only an acceptable but a desirable thing to do. It is now on the checklist for thousands of travelers to this great city.

Did it ever occur to you that someone had to seed this behavior in order for the idea to spread? Sure, plenty of people may well have been tempted to hold Juliet in suggestive ways, but someone had to be first. Probably more daring is the defacing of the walls in the piazza. Again, someone had to be first, and it takes more than a minute or two to engrave your initials into brick, even brick as old as this. I will bet you this was at first rejected by the local authorities. No question about it. In other words, the idea had to gain acceptance.

When you move the market, you need to acknowledge that at first there is ignorance. When you bring to light the new problem you are intending to solve, especially if the "problem" you are highlighting is the solution they are currently implementing to a different problem, that ignorance will likely be replaced by rejection.

You see, if your idea is at all innovative, it will challenge the status quo. This will put some people's noses out of joint. There is a lot invested in the status quo, and even when you are offering something better, the resistance to change or the fear of failure that can accompany it will be grounds to deny there is even a problem in the first place. Sometimes, it is jealousy, as some won't like the fact that you are the one who has come up with a better way and they would rather you didn't get the credit. This is often

119

manifested in companies at a cultural level as the "not invented here" syndrome, where new ideas that did not originate from within the company itself are rejected for the very reason that they were not invented inside its four walls. A culture has seemingly been built that leads its people to believe that only they are capable of developing good ideas.

Sounds petty, I know, but I have seen this cycle at the level of the individual, the team and even entire businesses.

Whenever you are presenting a new model of thinking, or even a new business model, it requires buyers to let go of their existing model. Depending on how successful this has been for them, depending on how they have built their identities around this role, and depending on how long they have been wedded to it, this could be hard or even seem impossible for them. And our job as a seller is to guide them through it as quickly and comfortably as possible, and to avoid reacting badly to certain parts of the process where the buyers' drive to defend rubs up against our idea.

Most new ideas require the rejection or at least enhancement of an old idea. As we have mentioned, that requires admitting there is something not quite right with the status quo. And this will ultimately take some accepting. It is crucial at this stage that you do not overtly set out to put the buyer in the wrong. Again, this is something I have personally done way too many times. And here is what I have found: when you suggest to the buyer that his or her model of the world is wrong, he or she does one of three things:

1. Rejects you and goes in search of a solution or a seller who shares his or her view of the world.
2. Attempts to convince you that you are wrong.
3. Realizes that he or she is wrong and seeks out anything that will rectify his or her situation.

You want the buyer to go for the third option, but in order to do so the buyer needs to feel as though he or she came to the conclusion, not you. Pushing your agenda in the face of someone who disagrees and giving his or her ideas no validation will almost guarantee that person will defend his or her model of the world.

The next competency of Influence will unpack various ways of getting around this problem, but I thought it important enough to mention here that even though you want to move the market, setting out to make everyone you encounter wrong is going to get you nowhere.

The point is, you should not be expecting to be met with open arms everywhere you go. Part of moving a market may require you to change it one buyer at a time. You may literally need to go door to door, winning over buyers one by one, until a critical mass of buyers supports your idea and it becomes the accepted wisdom of the market—in much the same way that fondling a statue is the "appropriate" thing to do in fair Verona.

It would be a real shame if you were to give up in the early phases of ignorance and rejection. Some of the great minds have felt the rejection of their ideas. Scientific journals rejected one of Stephen Hawking's original papers on black-hole radiation. Fred Smith all but failed on his

121

college paper outlining the business plan for what would later become FedEx. After doing some research, I found no fewer than 20 scientific articles that were initially rejected by the journals, the writers of which articles were eventually awarded the Nobel Prize for the very same piece of rejected work. Moving the market is what the great innovators, researchers and entrepreneurs do. You should never shy away from starting your revolution.

What I am really trying to say is "hold your nerve." Believe in what you offer and stay strong. Don't let a few rejections knock you off course. The rejections are part of the process, and the good thing about rejection is that you are at least one step closer to getting accepted. Or, from the mouth of a revolutionary herself, the anthropologist Margaret Mead, "Never underestimate the power of a small group of committed citizens to change the world. Indeed, it is the only thing that ever has." There is no reason why you cannot be the one who forms that group.

122

MAKING POSITIONING HAPPEN

▶ Always respect the mental barrier.

▶ Take a risk and stop trying to be everything to everyone. Instead, get very sharp in what you are offering. Even consider narrowing the markets you want to sell to.

▶ Remember that freedom follows focus and that specialization is not a dirty word.

▶ Develop a series of succinct and clear statements that describe your offer and the value it brings.

▶ Identify and accentuate what differentiates your offer, to the point of making it an obsession. Also, remember that what you are trying to hide in your background and experience may well be your most potent point of difference.

▶ Find the pain points of your buyers and home in on them. Then "spin" your language to align your offer with these problems and their solutions.

▶ Make sure your offer is on a positively growing trend and get in early as a lead solutions provider in that space—even if your solution is to an old problem. Find the latest trend for talking about the age-old problem.

▶ If need be, start the trend yourself and create the need by offering it, forcing it, seeding it, naming it, branding it, spreading it, uncovering it or maybe eventing it.

▶ Hold your nerve in the face of rejection.

▶ Return to packaging and start again if it really isn't working.

COMPETENCY
3

INFLUENCE

INFLUENCE CONVINCES THE BUYER TO
BUY WHAT HE OR SHE NEEDS
FROM YOU, NOW!

■

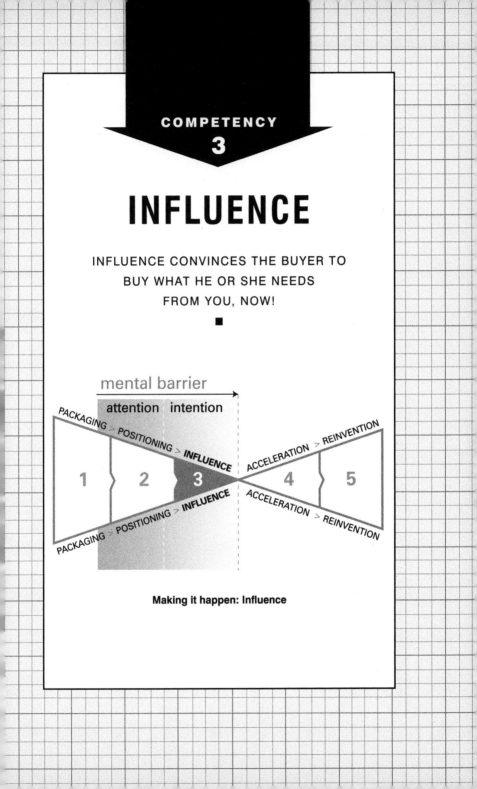

mental barrier

attention   intention

PACKAGING > POSITIONING > **INFLUENCE**

1   2   3   ACCELERATION > REINVENTION   4   5

PACKAGING > POSITIONING > **INFLUENCE**   ACCELERATION > REINVENTION

Making it happen: Influence

8

STORIES
AND STUFF:
POSITIONING 2.0

INFLUENCE REQUIRES THAT you do three things extremely well:

1. Take the buyer from being interested in your offer to committed to acquiring it. In order to do this, you need not only to align your offer to the obvious public (market) needs of the buyer (easy to need), giving him or her reasonable public support (easy to support), but also to align it to the buyer's personal wants (easy to want) and the buyer's need to justify his or her own behavior (easy to justify).

2. Convince the buyer to choose you. In other words, ensure that you (the seller) are easy to believe and easy to like.

3. **Make it easy to make the exchange.** Or, put simply, you need to make your offer easy to choose, easy to buy and easy to integrate.

It is no mistake that influence has been called an art. When it is done well, it is nothing short of a masterpiece. And it is quite possibly the most crucial competency to master. With all the talk we have engaged in so far, all the ideas we have discussed around packaging and positioning, the fact of the matter is we haven't sold anything yet. Influencing someone to actually exchange his or her time, money, credibility, power, energy or whatever it is you are seeking lies at the heart of making it happen.

All too often, we fall down at this point. We fail to close the deal. Remember, your success on the road to making it happen will not be judged by whether or not you had a well-packaged offer. It will not be judged by whether or not your offer satisfied a genuine market need. It will be judged by how many people you commit to the exchange. It will be judged by how many deals you were able to close. Or, as I said back in Chapter 1, if the way to Carnegie Hall is practice, practice, practice, then the way to making it happen is sell, sell, sell.

There is no shortage of recognized market needs for which buyers are nevertheless unwilling to exchange anything of value to see satisfied. And worse, even if you can get a buyer committed to an exchange, you need to ensure he or she enters into the exchange with you. And this is a far more delicate and complex thing to achieve than it may at first seem.

But it is achievable if we can understand four things:

1. Stories and stuff: How humans make decisions.
2. The buyer: What the buyer really wants/needs.
3. The seller: What you need to do/be to make him or her want it from you.
4. The sale: How to remove the barriers to exchange.

Closing the deal requires you to move another human being to make a decision—not just in his or her mind but carried through to his or her actions too. And in order to do this you need to understand how humans make decisions. At ChangeLabs we run some of largest behavioral change programs on earth, so understanding how human make decisions has become an obsession for us. To be honest, this topic could fill many books, so in an attempt to make it simple to understand, and more importantly simple to execute, I am going to give a very simple explanation to an extremely complex set of ideas and theories.

The good news is that neuroscience and behavioral psychology offer more answers to this question than we have ever had access to before. And some of what we have found out has shaken the very foundations of economic theory—most notably, the assumption that humans are rational beings. Just because your offer makes sense for a certain buyer to engage with, it does not mean

Closing the deal requires you to move another human being to make a decision.

that he or she will. As it turns out, research suggests that more than 90 percent of all human decisions are driven by emotions, but that we use our cognitive faculties to rationalize those emotional decisions to make them acceptable in the eyes of the people we want to be accepted by. I call the emotions the "story" and the rationalizations the "stuff." What's more is that when we try to give the justification for why we made a decision, we engage in what psychologists call introspective illusion, where we cannot accurately give reasons for why we did something and generally fabricate them. There is debate about whether we have the self-awareness to even know what our stories are or whether we all just have them at a mostly unconscious level, and make up "stuff" to feel better about the decisions we make.

Consider ice hockey as a fascinating example of how insane we can actually be. Ice hockey has a history dating back to the 1700s. However, it is generally regarded as having become an organized sport with widely accepted rules in 1886, when a formal game was played between Queen's University and the Royal Military College of Canada. It is a fabulously entertaining sport, as players skate rapidly from one end of the rink to the other with flailing sticks, sharp blades on their feet and a hard rubber puck flying through the air and along the ice at an average of 98 miles per hour.

Can you imagine what it must have been like in those early days to be a goaltender in the midst of all this chaos? Dangerous and scary are words that come to mind. Now, I have no problem understanding the absence of any facial protection for the goaltender for the 40 years from 1886 to 1926, because no one knew there was such a thing— not just in hockey but in any sport at that time. It is what happened after 1927 that shocks me most and offers tremendous insight into human behavior.

In 1927, one Elizabeth Graham wore a full-faced fiber-glass fencer's mask during a game for Queen's University. It obviously caused quite a stir and, when asked why she wore it (as though that was not obvious), she responded by saying it protected her teeth. The next recorded player to wear one was Clint Benedict, three years later. Benedict had been hit in the face in a game against the New York Americans in February 1930 and suffered a broken nose. On his return six weeks later, he was wearing a leather mask with a nose piece. After sporting it for five full games to protect his face, he stopped wearing it, claiming that it obscured his vision.

Do you think that was actually true? Do you think Benedict would have continued to wear the mask if it did not obscure his vision? Now, before you answer, I want you to think about something. What is the culture of ice hockey? How would you describe the "identity" of a professional hockey player? I bet "tough" would be one of the words that would come to mind. Maybe even "crazy." How do you think Clint Benedict would have been perceived had he been the first and only male player in professional hockey to wear protection for his face? What stigma would have surrounded that decision?

Now, I know I am making pretty big assumptions, but consider this. Even though a number of advancements were made in the years following 1930, and many different types of mask became available—including the all-in-one fiberglass mask that Elizabeth Graham had worn—not one single NHL player started to wear them. That was in spite of the fact that many had begun wearing them at training. It was a full 29 years later before a player decided to consistently wear one in real match environments. And the story that surrounded that decision is equally revealing.

Jacques Plante had taken a liking to the fiberglass mask. In fact, he had taken a liking to the concept of facial protection for goalies full stop. He had worked hard in his own time off the ice to develop protective equipment and would later be credited with completely changing the way goaltenders kept goal as a result of his willingness to wear protective clothing.

Jacques wore his mask full-time at training during his time with the Montreal Canadiens. His coach, Toe Blake, however, refused to let him wear it in a game. Why? Well, according to Toe, it would "impair Jacques' vision." But not according to Jacques himself. And it is not as if Jacques' performance was suspect. So good in fact was Jacques Plante that in 1956–57 Blake refused to give any game time to back-up goalie Gerry McNeil and in the end McNeil went to play for the Royals. In the years that followed, Jacques, Blake and the Canadiens went on to win five Stanley Cups. (Plante missed more than a few play-off games during this time due to injury.)

And then it happened: the showdown that is now hockey legend. On November 1, 1959, Andy Bathgate of the New York Rangers struck Plante in the face with the puck, opening him up. After being stitched up, Plante refused to return to the ice without the mask. He had had enough. He had taken one too many pucks to the head and insisted on being able to protect himself. Blake resisted initially, but when Plante held firm the thought of losing the match to forfeit because he had no goalie was too great a price to pay.

132

Plante had obviously decided that having his facial features and teeth intact when he ceased playing was more important than being seen as tough. Toe obviously had other things on his mind. He was widely respected both as a player and as a coach, and his reputation was built on his toughness, reflected in the way that he played, the way that he trained and the way that he pushed his teams to higher standards. In other words, his entire story was built on being tough, and there was no way one of his players was going to tarnish that reputation by wearing some wretched mask. The mask was a symbol of weakness and flew in the face of the identity that Toe Blake had constructed for himself.

Many goaltenders owe their front teeth to Plante and his act of courage. You see, it wasn't just Toe Blake who had forged an identity of toughness; it was the entire NHL. For three decades, protective options had been available to these players and none had chosen to take them up. The story of being "tough" was too powerful— even in the face of a reality that meant regular concussions, stitching, and broken facial bones. And the reason given for their unwillingness was always that masks impaired their vision. But not enough to stop them wearing them at training!

Today, things are obviously very different. The story that would be told now about someone playing professional hockey without a mask is that he is an idiot. Change the story and you change the behavior.

Now, you may be wondering why we are revisiting the competency of Positioning in the title of this chapter (Stories and Stuff: Positioning 2.0). Well, in its truest sense, influence is an act of positioning. You influence the buyer by positioning your offer in a way that aligns with his or her personal wants/needs and positioning yourself as the right person to buy from in his or her mind.

In fact, it is not just influence and positioning that are very closely interrelated in this book, but the first three of its competencies, including packaging. You have probably already realized that decisions you make in packaging your idea are in fact acts of positioning it with a market need, and many of the strategies from the Positioning competency have laid the groundwork for this competency, Influence. When you are fully familiar with all three of these concepts, I hope you will find yourself using them simultaneously, with each informing the others. To enable you to gain mastery, though, I have set them out here as three separate concepts.

What truly differentiates Influence from the previous two competencies is that it removes your thinking from the abstract world of offers and ideas and places it firmly in the world of human interaction.

People buy from people. Period. And we buy from people we either like or want to be like. In my experience, a second-rate offer from a master influencer has a better chance of being bought than a great offer from a poor influencer.

We will now set out on a journey of discovery about what really makes someone buy—and, more importantly, buy from you. Perhaps I shouldn't say this, but this is my favorite competency of the book. Some of the ideas in here sit at the heart of what I so dearly want to share with you. I have seen too many people work too hard to make it happen only to fall short because they lack the skills to close the deal. Unfortunately, this can come down to simple things such as how confident you are, how prepared you are to say no and push back when a buyer tries to get the upper hand, and even how you dress and present yourself. I hope you enjoy what follows as much as I have enjoyed writing it.

To be a master of influence requires that we can simultaneously be aware of the market need and understand and position ourselves (and our offer) to meet the individual buyer's needs. The buyer is not a market. The buyer is a human. And while every buyer has responsibilities to his or her family and organization, he or she will inevitably act out of self-interest every time he or she buys. Your job is to work out what the buyer's personal hot buttons are and zero in on them, demonstrating how your offer can help the buyer to get more of what he or she personally wants, avoid more of what he or she personally wants to avoid and get closer to who he or she aspires to be. Or, put differently, influence is personal positioning.

You see, every product someone buys, every service someone engages and every company or individual someone chooses to buy from makes a statement about that person (in this case as a buyer), both to himself or herself and to the world.

It may be useful to know that the word "position" comes from the marketing concept that every product occupies a "space" in the mind of the buyer. And that the buyer "positions" each offer based on the benefits and features that offer presents. For instance, Harley-Davidson might hold the "position" in your mind as the brand

135

to buy when you want the world to know you are in charge of your destiny, that you will not be dictated to.

Now, if you were to ask a Harley rider why he doesn't ride, say, a BMW motorbike, which many would argue will get you to the same place in more comfort and with fewer mechanical challenges, he would say it is because BMWs are not "the real deal." The BMW does not have the history, or the 45-degree V-twin engine for which Harleys are famous. Some may suggest that BMWs are for wimps.

The real reason why people ride Harleys is that it makes them feel rebellious. They have a deep yearning for the sense of freedom that comes with owning and riding a Harley and being on the open road. They use features such as the engine and the history to justify this highly emotional decision. In other words, they have a "story" that drives their behavior and a whole lot of "stuff" they draw upon to justify their emotional decision.

Or what about an equally telling example, but from a market segment you would expect to be much more rational in its purchasing behavior: engaging an IT solutions provider? Why do people hire IBM? Well, as the old saying goes, no one gets fired for hiring IBM.

People don't engage IBM just because it might be the best company when it comes to integrating your technology solutions; they buy IBM because the brand has such power and such history that there is no chance of you getting fired for using it. Never mind if you could get the same service or product elsewhere, potentially even for less. The personal fear of being exposed by taking a risk on a smaller player is not worth it. This may seem rational on an individual level, but it is not really rational on a business level. Of course, you can't say to your boss, "I hired IBM because I was scared of making a mistake." But in truth this is partly why the company is so massive.

Interestingly enough, this tide is turning and increasingly people are opting for smaller IT providers because of their agility and personal service. Indeeed, our perpetual example, Salesforce.com, used this very same risk-free strategy to convince buyers to make the switch online.

The Salesforce.com business model is such that you pay monthly licenses, to use the software. You don't need to sink huge amounts of capital into the software itself—although you do to customize it to your sales process—so you are not contracted to stay with the product, and you have less of an opportunity cost for making the switch back. It is as close to risk free as it can be, with the exception of Salesforce.com offering to refund any third party developer costs you have may incurred.

So, when it comes to trying to close the deal with a buyer, it is important to know what features and benefits (stuff) you should emphasize about your offer. And this all depends on what type of story you are trying to align your offer to.

Only by knowing that the Harley-Davidson buyer wants to feel rebellious and free does the company make its decision to connect its brand with fringe activities such as the Ultimate Fighting Championship. Only by knowing that an IT services buyer is paranoid about losing his job because he made the wrong decision do you know to focus on history, size and track record.

Consider one last example: imagine you are offering your services as a business coach. In this case, it is key to know that not only is the buyer motivated by the chance to make more money but also he may in fact just be grateful that he no longer feels alone on the entrepreneurial journey. It is well understood that being a CEO and an entrepreneur is a lonely road, and many of the powerful mentoring and coaching networks that exist for CEOs are popular not because of the content of the monthly briefings but because of the sense of camaraderie the CEO gets from knowing that he or she is not the only one going through it.

You need to know this when you are selling your coaching services, because the decision of which coach to engage (assuming you are not the only one in the market) may come down to who they like the most, and not who had the prettiest brochure. In this instance, you may choose to avoid using the sales language of a brochure altogether and insist on a face-to-face meeting with the buyer. This will be the first step in addressing the desire to connect at human level that the buyer so desperately is seeking. That is not to say you won't need to ensure that the buyer can justify the decision to engage you through your proven ability to increase profits. It is just that the latter justification is not the only reason to engage a coach, and it may be the case that the only reason the buyer engaged you as his or her coach was the private desire to have a friend on the journey and that they liked you. In other words, you design your sales process around meeting the private as well as the public drives of the buyer. It is not one or the other; it is both. However, in my experience, it starts with the private and you design outwards. Not the other way around.

Let me sum up:

- Stuff: the justifications for why you make a particular decision.
- Story: the real drivers behind the decision.
- Base your "stuff" on the "story" you are trying to sell.

And herein lies the first step to becoming more influential. You must take your mastery of positioning and make it personal. Don't just attempt to align your offer with an explicit market need; you need to align it to the implicit needs of the individual buyers within that market. And it is for this reason that we now direct our attention towards better understanding the buyer, and identifying the powerful forces behind the stories that drive buyers' behavior.

9

THE BUYER

IF INFLUENCE IS taking our positioning and making it personal, then it is essential to understand the buyer in all his or her human complexity. This should be fun!

I want you to imagine you are in a room with 50 other people. You have all showed up for what you expect will be a fairly dry information evening about a job opportunity. Only dry it is not. There is not a dry eye in the place. Tears are streaming down your face as you listen to a boy with a serious physical disability tell you how he has just graduated from high school, and that the only reason he made it this far in his life was the love and support of a social worker, who is sitting just two rows in front of you. She is obviously bawling too, and gets up to share with the room how much she loves her job and the sense of meaning she gets when she does it.

You, on the other hand, cannot help but think of how meaningless your job seems in comparison—you work as an administrative assistant at a coal mine some 40 minutes out of town. You are so moved by what you are seeing that you feel compelled to leave your current job and start working in community services. I, meanwhile, am sitting at the back of the room, thinking, "Yes! Another convert to my idea."

This is a true story. I once worked on an employer-branding project for a community-services organization that was trying to attract people to work with kids with disabilities. By employer branding, I mean building a positive association around the organization and the opportunities it provided for potential talent. It was right in the middle of the massive mining boom, and the organization was situated just one hour from three of the biggest coal mining sites in the world. Needless to say, anyone with a heartbeat was already employed and paid handsomely to dig up and transport dirt.

My client had been running ads for months on every website and in every paper it could. Most times, it got not one application. The reason: its ads sucked. The organization listed loads of criteria as compulsory, even though in reality all of the required skills could be attained very quickly and cheaply once on the job. The ads were full of very clinical and bureaucratic language, and in order to apply you had to jump through a series of hoops and supply more paperwork than would accompany a U.S. immigration form. As if that was not enough, the outfit highlighted in its advertising what was tough about the job, with little reference to what was good—a sure-fire way to be neither noticeable nor compelling. The first thing I did was change the ad.

It used to read, "Qualified professionals required to work in the disability sector." Now it read, "Are you sick of coming home from work each day knowing you did not make a meaningful difference?" We also ran variations on this theme, such as, "How would you like to go to bed at night knowing someone's life was better because you went to work that day?" And, when space was more limited, "How would you like to have a job that matters?"

This time, instead of asking them to express interest and supply reams of documentation, we simply invited them to an information evening the following week. We know anecdotally and from research that people are more emotional when they are in a group. And if you think back to the last chapter you now know that more than 90 percent of all decisions are emotionally driven. The larger the group, the more intense the collective emotional experience.

The Journal of Consumer Research suggests that, over the course of a film, movie-watchers influence one another and gradually synchronize their emotional responses. This mutual mimicry also affects each participant's evaluation of the overall experience—the more in synch we are with the people around us, the more we like the movie. People laugh longer and cry more when they are in a group. Hollywood knows this. And people who want to make it happen need to know it as well.

My client's desire was to increase its staff. What this actually translated to was getting someone to leave a job paying twice the money, to work longer hours in a much

142

more challenging role. I knew the only way this could ever happen is if I got people so emotionally moved that they switched off the rational parts of their brains, in pursuit of a greater sense of significance. And I knew the only way I could make that happen was to create an experience where everyone in the room felt bonded and collectively moved. I needed to use a form of positive peer pressure, and I needed to take them on a journey through the real-life stories of people whose lives had been changed.

We got almost 50 people to the information evening— twice as many as we had hoped for in our wildest dreams. I had arranged for two social workers to share their experiences of working for this organization and the great sense of meaning it brought them, and I also brought in two of the "clients," who had achieved great things in spite of their disabilities.

The client you have already heard about was the last to speak. As you know, he explained how he had just finished high school and that there was no way he or his family could have done it without the help of the social worker employed by the organization we were recruiting for.

And it was immediately after this, with tears still in the audience's eyes, that the organization asked if anyone would be interested in applying. In fact, it went one step further and locked people into an interview as soon as humanly possible after that evening.

I have been accused of being manipulative when I do these sorts of things, especially when we used the young boy with a disability. But I reject the notion entirely. The community of disabled kids in the region where we did

143

this project are now much better served than they were prior. And I know that the people who took the job must have been glad about their decision, because I am told that to date not one has left. We did not lie about the pay or working hours, we merely emphasized the positive and used group psychology in our favor.

Influence is ultimately about manipulation, but doing it for good is noble and not deceitful. It is motive that makes the difference.

If you cannot get a buyer excited enough to engage with your idea, you have no chance of ever turning that good idea into a positive result. And if you want to know how to move people, how to incite certain behaviors, you need to know what drives them. If you know what motivates them, and you can align yourself and your offer to that drive, you will become very easy to want. You unleash your power to influence when you make your offer (and indeed yourself) easy to want.

EASY TO WANT

Humans have basic drives. Both Positioning and Influence attempt to tap in to these deep human drives. What we need to know is can we define these drives, and can they help us package our offer and direct our behavior in a way that speaks to them and gets the buyer excited enough to buy? The answers are yes and yes!

For decades, psychologists and sociologists, and more recently neurologists, have tried to put their fingers on the drivers of human behavior. For fear of putting you to sleep,

144

I will not track the history of thinking in this area but rather start with one of the most modern and, I believe, applicable interpretations of the collective research in this area.

Dr. P. R. Lawrence and his colleagues have done some fascinating work in the field of human behavior. They have published various books on the subject, including *Driven: How Human Nature Shapes Our Choices*. In June 2008, a very popular article appeared in the *Harvard Business Review* with compelling empirical evidence to support their theory. What they suggest is that there are four omnipresent human drives, which have been deeply ingrained in us through evolution.

Rather than constantly referring back to Lawrence and his colleagues, let me be very clear here that the theoretical underpinnings of what I am about to share come from their work. I suggest you visit www.prlawrence.com for more information on their research.

Let me give you a quick overview of the four drives and then unpack each of them in some detail, with attention placed on how you can tap in to them when trying to influence a buyer.

- **Drive to acquire:** We seek to acquire scarce goods, services and experiences that bolster our sense of well-being and elevate our social status.
- **Drive to bond:** We seek to connect on an emotional level with other people, brands or causes.
- **Drive to comprehend:** We seek to understand our world, and assign meaning to things.
- **Drive to defend:** We seek to protect that which we already have, including ourselves, our posses-

145

sions, our friends and families and the things we believe in.

The more you can satisfy these drives, and the more of them you can satisfy simultaneously, the more compelled the buyer will be to actually engage.

In a session with the team at Sega, we spent a few hours going through all the mega-hit games of the last 20 years, and all of the ones we could think of appealed to at least three of the four fundamental human drives. It was as though the creators had deliberately set out to tap in to these drives in the design phase, and then the communities that were built around the various games helped reinforce them and a sort of addiction ensued.

Now, you may feel like adding other drives here, but I would challenge you to find one that was not a derivative of these four. The drive for growth, for instance, is a combination of the drive to comprehend and the drive to acquire. The death drive that Freud refers to in his work about our desire to stave off change and create peace and order has elements of both the drive to defend (as in, to maintain the calm and certainty of the status quo) and the drive to comprehend (in order to be satisfied with your existing model of the world).

It is important to realize that these drives are independent of each other and can also be in conflict. A manager may make a decision that satisfies his drive to acquire but will have a negative impact on some of his peers, and thus will be in conflict with his drive to bond. The brain has developed phenomenal tools for rationalizing these con-

146

flicts away, allowing us to perceive a harmony between our behaviors and our drives. As humans, we find it highly uncomfortable to feel an incongruence between different desires, and, worse, between what we say matters to us and what our behavior suggests really matters to us.

This will become clearer as we move through, and will reveal itself as a key lever for compelling the buyer into action. For now, though, all I really want you to get is that the more powerfully you can connect to these private drives (acquire, bond, comprehend and defend), the more likely it is you will be able to compel the individual buyer to engage with you and your offering.

Drive to Acquire

When is enough enough? As it turns out, never. Our evolutionary drive to acquire resources that are needed for our survival is so deeply ingrained in us that, even though we have no problem "surviving" in modern Western societies, the fundamental need to ensure we have more is still with us.

This is why I am always fascinated when people say money doesn't motivate. Wrong! Sure, it does not make you happy, but money is a core part of the modern expression of the drive to acquire and has been ever since societies developed a currency for the exchange of scarce resources. Money is both the means to an end and an end in itself.

The drive to acquire manifests itself in two different types of "goods" that we seek:

147

1. **Regular goods:** These are items that are part of our need for survival. They include food, water, clothes, housing, sex, and even entertainment.
2. **Positional goods:** These are the items that confer status or social recognition.

Which is your offer? Does your proposition best fulfill a regular desire or a positional one? It is worth thinking about.

The desire for regular goods is one that is easily understood. In modern society, much of these are taken care of, and there are few people deprived of them to a point that they no longer survive.

It is for this reason that we turn our attention to the concept of positional desire. The drive to acquire is measured by humans in a relative, rather than an absolute, sense. In other words, we are more concerned with, "Do we have more than the person next to us?" than, "Do we have enough?" Experiments have shown this time and time again.

Imagine you have the choice of living in one of two worlds, A and B, with identical prices and costs of living. In world A, you will earn $90,000 and your neighbor will earn $100,000.

In world B, you will earn $110,000 and your neighbor will earn $200,000.

Which world do you want to live in?

As it turns out, the most common answer is A, even though in financial terms you would be better off in world B. We prefer the first world because we would be closer in status to our neighbor.

This is why people always say you need to emphasize what's in it for the buyer. What good, product or experience will you offer that is both scarce and desirable? And, if you really want to have a powerful influence over the buyer, you need to figure out how your offer can present them with the opportunity to be and do more, relative to their peer group.

Now, stop shaking your head in denial. Sure, you and your friends may have no desire to "beat" the people around you in terms of your acquisition of money and material possessions. But before you reject or deny this model of the world, stop and realize that I did not say it had to be money or material possessions. In academia, the drive to acquire may manifest itself by counting the number of citations one has received or the instances of being published. In a church, it may be by totaling the time one has spent in service to that particular church or by the donations one has made.

Even if your reaction was, "I am not like this. I don't care that much about acquisition," well, that very thought is the drive to acquire, as it suggests you think it is better to not have that thought, as though you have a moral superiority over those who do. I am not judging here, merely trying to point out that we all have this drive and that it is in play all the time.

The main thing to realize is that the kind of social standing, the kind of experiences and the kind of goods people want differ depending on their definition of what is important. It may be money, it may be philanthropy, it may even be fitness levels or tennis ability (the last one is alive and well in my Wisteria Lane-like

149

neighborhood in Colorado). The drive is present in all of us; it just manifests itself in different ways. For instance, have you seen the explosion of reusable bags for shopping? These bags are flaunted by many as status symbols themselves. Similarly, when I lived in LA, there were as many people advertising their identity by driving a Prius as there were by driving a Ferrari. The Prius people want to show that they are more environmentally friendly than the person next to them. The Ferrari owners are trying to show they are wealthier or more suave than the person next to them.

In other words, the drive to acquire does not have be rooted in opulence, but in whatever is required to advance someone's sense of survival, well-being and social standing in the group they choose to bond with.

So let's now apply this to our quest to make it happen through considering business coaching. The buyer is obviously going to be interested in making his or her business more successful—in other words, in making more money through greater revenue or lower costs. Appealing to this need will be a powerful reason for engaging a coach. But you also need to encourage the buyer to engage you as that coach. You could do this by demonstrating that he or she will make more money by engaging with you than with any of your competitors. You could follow that with details of your policy not to work with more than one business in any one industry so you can ensure maximum competitive advantage for the buyer. You could also gently mention that you are meeting with one of the buyer's competitors, and should the buyer desire your services exclusively he or she would need to engage you in the next few days. And, from a brand perspective, you could position yourself as only working with six businesses at any one time, meaning you would need to consider the buyer's "application" to work with you very carefully. Then, when he or she engages you, you can emphasize how he or she is the only person in his or her industry to have access to your insights.

You will sense here that, in addition to competition, fear has a large part to play in people's motivation. This is true. Fear, from a "drive to acquire" perspective, comes from the fact that food, goods and resources are in fact scarce and that the competitive market (which for many can mean life and death) is a zero-sum game. The market is not, as many suggest, abundant. There will be winners and there will be losers. The reason why scarcity is so powerful is that if something is scarce, we run the risk of our neighbor having it instead of us, which not only presents us with the problem of being lower in social status but, at a deep, unconscious level, also challenges our very survival. Hence, people seem to act "irrationally" in pursuit of that which is rare.

Buyers want to be best, or at least better.

In closing, let me say this: buyers want to be first. Buyers want to be best, or at least better. They want more power, more influence, bigger budgets and a greater chance to make an impact themselves. They want to be significant. You need to show them, or imply to them, that engaging with you and your idea will offer them the opportunity to do just that.

151

Here are five things you should consider when trying to influence buyers that can help tap in to their drive to acquire:

1. Communicate clearly what is in it for them.
2. Show how your offer will help them outdo their competition.
3. Create a sense of exclusivity in your offer.
4. Avoid appearing desperate, else there will be no sense of scarcity.
5. Where appropriate, you may mention that you are talking to their competitors about the same opportunity.

Drive to Bond

With the drive to acquire comes a seemingly conflicting desire to bond. Only two days ago, I was looking at a billboard advertising a very hip line of clothing with the tagline "blend out." The pictured model was wearing a white suit with lime-green-patterned shirt and shoes. I don't think he would have too many problems blending out. Our drive to acquire makes us want to stand out, but our drive to bond makes sure we don't stand out too much. Life is full of paradoxes, don't you think?

The desire to connect is a drive that comes from both the biological reality of being a human and the way we have developed in our societies. The fact that we depend on our mothers for survival for a much longer period than other animals and the fact that we have created role specialization in our societies make it essential that we can bond and cooperate with others, in order to live.

152

There is so much tied in to our drive to bond. It goes beyond just wanting to be a part of a family or to have friends. We want to see ourselves as part of something bigger. We attach ourselves to brands and to companies that we believe represent who we are, or at least who we want to be. It is like a progression. We start with a pairing (think mother and child, or husband and wife), we move to a face-to-face group (think your inner circle of friends), then to social networks (your outer circle of friends and acquaintances, such as your work colleagues) and then on to collectives (such as organizations, nations, fan bases and brand users).

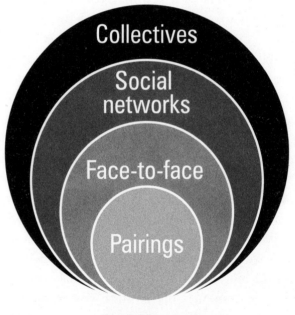

Progressional bonds

Interestingly, the beginning of the bonding process is believed to be tied to eye contact, touching, talking and sharing food. This poses an interesting challenge in the geographically spread nature of so much of what we do now, but it shows you why websites such as Facebook are so popular. Facebook is not about wasting time, or avoiding moments of boredom; it is fundamentally about bonding with other people. It is richer than email, in terms of the experiences it offers, as it can include live chat, the sharing of images and the sharing of symbols.

I often joke about the East Village in Manhattan. It is where many alternative, anti-institutional people live and hang out. There are many different shades of hair color, more piercings than at a Marilyn Manson concert, and enough emos to make you want to run and hide. Yet, what I find so amusing is that they all live together in the same suburb, going to the same restaurants and coffee shops, reading the same street publications. In fact, the anti-consumerist brand has become a very powerful consumer brand indeed. The desire to disconnect from society is simultaneously and conversely a deep desire to bond with others who feel the same way and like the same things. And this desire is so deep that we will literally all move to the same area.

However, it is not just other people who we want to bond with. We also want to be associated with brands and causes. Have you met an Apple user lately? It is as though they are members of a cult. Apple has such a powerful bond with its customers, due mostly to its commitment to design and simplicity, that its users would happily pay more for its products. The best evidence of this at Apple is the number of people who attend, or watch online, the keynotes of legendary founder Steve Jobs. People want to

154

belong, and they are happy to belong to a group of brand enthusiasts. They will, in many cases, buy something just because it is Apple. Think 3 million iPads in the first 6 months. Surely, there really weren't 3 million people who needed a tablet computing device. But there were 3 million people wanting to be cool and on the edge.

An obvious example of the drive to bond can be found in the fan bases of sporting franchises. Don't you find it fascinating that even a perpetually bad team can still have a loyal fan base? It is almost as though the pain of losing is outweighed by the benefit of sharing in the pain together.

In a slightly more negative manifestation, the drive to bond gives birth to an "us and them" mentality. When we move on to the discussion of you, the seller, and being easy to like, you will quickly discover how important it is to be one of "us," at least in the mind of the buyer. It is very normal to try to categorize and discriminate against people, including you the seller, and you could very quickly find yourself on the wrong side of this distinction.

Now, the secret here is not to try to translate this too literally. I wouldn't, for instance, rock up to a meeting with a buyer and say, "Buy this and you will be cool like me." Nor would an edgy fashion brand such as G-Star RAW say, "Wear this and you won't look like a loser." It is more subtle than that—subtle, sure, but no less powerful.

Indeed, you do want the buyer to think, "If I buy from this person, I will be more than I was before and I will be part of a group of people to which I aspire to belong." If you think about it, this is exactly what politicians do when trying to win an election. A good politician will be able to "name" an issue of social importance

155

and then, using rhetoric and sometimes policy, unite a group of people who agree with the politician's position on this issue and in turn vote for him or her.

Perhaps the best example of using the drive to bond comes from around the corner from my Sydney offices, at Deus motorcycles. Dare Jennings—the brand builder famed for creating Mambo—kicked this off when he recognised that the surfer bikie culture of the '60s had vanished in Australia yet was still alive in Japan. He imported the style and sensibilities of the "Japanese greaser" (greaser is not a derogatory term in this context but rather refers to a youth subculture that was traditionally more into cars but shared a love of old-style Triumph motorbikes) into Australia with his Deus Ex Machina. This bike shop basically builds custom motorcycles—all of which are quite classic machines. It calls it "chopping," based on the original Harley-Davidson Choppers of Oakland, California.

You may recognize the name. Deus Ex Machina was a personification of the machines that controlled the matrix in the later part of *The Matrix Revolutions.* The term itself is of Latin origin and means "god in the machine." It refers back to Greek dramas where a seemingly impossible problem was solved by a deity turning up out of the blue (as if jumping out of a box) to make it all better.

Anyway, this bike-chopping shop not only created a revenue stream for custom bikes but also launched (or should I say relaunched) an anti-establishment youth culture almost overnight. It sells clothes and all sorts of other non-motorcycle apparel and is fast becoming a powerful Aussie brand. Its rapid success can be attributed to Jennings's abil-

156

ity to establish a "collective" that perfectly aligned itself to the desires of anti-establishment Sydney youth.

As a side note, the drive to acquire is not always separate from the drive to bond. In a study done at Duke University by Michael Platt, it was shown that monkeys, and it seems humans too, will pay more to look at a fellow monkey of higher social standing (measured in willingness to part with fruit juice) than to look at a monkey who was considered lower on the social scale in that monkey community. In other words, we prefer to see ourselves aligned with people of higher social standing than with those of lower. Or, put more bluntly, we are snobs—even if our snobbery is towards social consciousness rather than material acquisition.

The opportunity to hang out with the "right" kind of people is a compelling proposition for humans, and you can position your offer in a way that suggests it will afford the buyer an opportunity to be surrounded by people your buyer in some way aspires to be like, or to be liked by. Better still, you need to represent that person yourself. No one wants to deal with a loser. There will be more on this later.

And the same will work in reverse. If positioning is a discriminatory activity, then the brands, groups and symbols you distance yourself from are in many ways as powerful as those you attempt to align yourself with. In other words, who you don't bond with is as important as who you do. What you don't do in pursuit of a buyer can be as powerful as what you do. Buyers respect confidence, unless of course that confidence threatens their alpha status. Again, we will revisit this later, when we discuss identity.

Here are five things you should consider doing when trying to appeal to the buyer's drive to bond:

1. Show what kind of person you are, and what sort of people you are surrounded by. Don't be afraid to stand for something, and don't check your personality at the door. Confidence is especially powerful and attractive.
2. Present yourself in such a way that a buyer might aspire to be like you.
3. Listen intently so you can find out what the buyer values and what you share in common.
4. Meet in person and share a meal where possible.
5. Be as interested in the buyer, and his or her world, as you are in making the sale.

And, just quickly before I move on, the kind of person a buyer responds to and aspires to emulate does not have to be rich and famous. We all manifest these human drives in unique ways, and the good news is that there are communities and tribes of all types around the world.

Drive to Comprehend

Has anyone ever handed you a toy that they were trying to figure out how to put together? Now, initially you may have had no interest in that toy, and you may even have been very busy to start with. However, the allure of solving the problem was so great that you just had to figure it out.

This happened to me the other day when my son handed me a Transformer. The toy was so complicated that despite 20 minutes of my best efforts I still could not get this thing to come together. Don't read this the wrong way. This was not 20 minutes of quality time with my son. This was 20 minutes of me deep in my own thoughts and actions, completely ignoring the fact that I was robbing my son of the opportunity to figure this out for himself. And this was not something that was going to enhance my life, my business or my family in any way whatsoever. It was a bloody Transformer, for Pete's sake.

So, did I figure it out? No. I just could not get it. I ended up convincing myself that there must have been a piece missing or that it was a poorly made toy. That was until I saw my nephew, barely five years old, do it in about three minutes flat. Not cool at all. What do you think happened? I went back to that same toy with even more intensity than the first time, only this time I was motivated by my need to "beat" my five-year-old nephew—in other words, by my drive to acquire. Sick, I know, but I got there in the end.

The first time I'd tried to figure it out, I was driven by something very different. I was driven by my need to, well . . . figure it out. This is known as the drive to comprehend, and it usually applies to tasks a little more important than transforming a Transformer.

I used to say that clarity sells—that is, people buy answers. As it turns out, this seems to be mostly right. The drive to comprehend reflects a deep need for humans to make sense of their world, to understand why things happen and what the purpose of their life is.

But it does not have to be as profound as this, as my example has suggested. We are equally engaged by learning

159

itself, and also by creation. People like to learn and they like to create, and they like to have a greater sense of clarity and meaning in their lives. You can tap in to this. In other words, you can sell answers, sure, but selling the opportunity to discover the answers for yourself can be just as alluring.

I think, more than ever, this is a drive that compels us in modern life. Our drive to acquire has been out of control in recent times, and I believe we have now begun to collectively ask the questions: What is this all for? What is the meaning of this? What is my life supposed to be about? We want to make more sense of our world, and our roles in it. So you need to stop and ask yourself, how does your proposition help people gain more answers? What answers does it give meaning to?

As it turns out, we are particularly interested in things that are a little novel—that is, things that don't quite fit our existing model of the world. An idea that presents a new perspective, and a new opportunity, should pique the interest of a buyer. That is, providing the seller does not attack the buyer's existing model, and the idea itself is not so far removed from the existing model that it seems scarcely imaginable.

And note, too, there is no way we will adopt a new belief system, or even just a new IT system, if we do not think it will be an improvement on the old one. Just being novel will get you through the attention barrier but most probably not through the intention barrier.

160

Consider this book. I have already asked you why you bought it. I know the answer. You bought it because it offered the promise of something more, the promise of pointers as to how you too can make it happen, the missing link, the life-changing insight (I hope you have found one).

It is estimated that in the U.S. alone, the self-help market is worth more than $10 billion. That is a lot of money being spent on books, CDs and seminars to satisfy people's drives to acquire and to comprehend. Of equal interest in these last few years has been the explosion in books on economic theory and neuroscience, with insights into how and why we do what we do: *Freakonomics, The Undercover Economist, Outliers,* just to name a few. These books offer novel and very interesting perspectives on our behavioral motivations. They incite the drive to comprehend and have been extremely popular for this reason.

Again it is for this reason, that despite being the CEO of ChangeLabs, I also deliver more than 100 presentations at conferences around the world each year. And even though I never sell from the platform—this would be insulting and disrespectful to the audience and the client who has invested in my attendance—the very act of sharing expertise and insight builds credibility for me and my company. 80% of our clients have come from audiences.

Lets see if Salesforce.com have done the same thing. A quick search of Mark Benioff will show you that he has published 3 books. Consider the titles here:

Compassionate Capitalism: How Corporations Can Make Doing Good an Integral Part of Doing Well, with Karen Southwick (2004)

The Business of Changing the World: 20 Great Leaders on Strategic Corporate Philanthropy, with Carlye Adler (2006)

*Behind the Cloud: The Untold Story of How Sales-
force.com Went from Idea to Billion-Dollar Company and Revolutionized an Industry*, with
Carlye Adler (2009)

All of these are books designed to both position Sales-
force.com and mark them as thought leaders, innovators,
and people who change the world. Who would not want
to have access to that sort of insight, and in the spirit of
the drive to bond, do business with a company that shares
those values?

Here are three things you should consider doing when
trying to influence the buyer that can help tap in to his or
her drive to comprehend:

1. Create a dialogue and elicit the buyer's point of
   view. See if you can bring him or her to the conclusion that your offer will solve his or her problems. Make it the buyer's idea!
2. Bring a unique perspective on the problem you
   are trying to solve for the buyer.
3. Co-create a solution to the buyer's problem. In
   other words, don't come up with all the answers.
   Actually engage in a process of creative synergy
   and come up with co-authored solutions (all of
   which involve your offer).

162   **Drive to Defend**

It makes for a great movie, doesn't it? The wife and family
of the hero taken hostage, hurt or even killed. And the

resulting rampage of the hero in defense of what he holds so dear. Think *Man on Fire*, think *Taken*, think *Braveheart*, think *The Patriot*, and on the list could go.

Why do you think these movies are so popular? Because they are stories that reach into the heart of an instinctual human drive: to defend what is ours. Whether it be protecting our wealth, securing our home or defending our country, this drive is something that affects us all, and something we are all willing to spend money on. Consequently, it offers ample opportunity to get the buyer engaged.

A simple example comes from Richard Branson. In his early days, and I mean when he was still a 16-year-old, he got his first breakthrough with a new (he had already started others) business trying to launch a magazine called *Student*. It was a free magazine, so it relied entirely on advertising for revenue. No one wanted to be a part of it, until one day Branson happened upon a strategy that perfectly aligned with people's need to defend what they have. He would ring Pepsi, tell it that Coca-Cola had just taken out a half-page ad on page 23 and that if it was quick (scarcity and fear of loss) he could give it a full-page ad on page 17. Pepsi, it turned out, would oblige, and then he would call Coca-Cola, which had not taken out an ad at all, and suggest that now that Pepsi was in there, it had better be too and he only had one slot left—a half-page on page 23.

It worked. This was his sales strategy—employed out of desperation, no doubt—but this magazine started what has become one of the most inspiring and celebrated entrepreneurial stories of modern times. And it was built

163

on the competitive nature of the drive to acquire and the desire to protect one's turf.

It is for this very reason that fear sells. Much has been said of former president George W. Bush and his administration's ability to use fear as a motivator. What I am about to say is not in any way a political statement, but rather to shine light on a very smart and effective strategy for influencing human behavior. The "axis of evil," the "war against terror," and "weapons of mass destruction" were all used to generate voter commitment. If people fear that their safety and quality of life are at risk, they will permit behavior that under other circumstances they would find unacceptable.

The events of 9/11 led to approval ratings that were near the highest of any president. Why? Because the 9/11 attacks set alight the drive to defend in almost all Americans. A very proud nation to begin with, this was all they needed to rally behind an attempt to "defend" the liberties they valued so dearly.

So, how can you appeal to people's drive to defend? Here are five things you should consider when trying to influence the buyer that can help tap in to his or her drive to defend:

1. Never attack the buyer's point of view.
2. Never criticize the way the buyer has done things to date.
3. Always communicate how you will protect the buyer from the inherent risk of loss in the exchange (money, credibility, job).
4. Don't be afraid to subtly mention the risks of not engaging with you.

164

5. Talk openly about the progress of the buyer's competitors.

In summary, understanding the four fundamental drives in all buyers is essential in making sure your offer is easy to want. The drives give you a short cut to tapping in to the private reasons for someone being willing to engage, as opposed to just the public ones, and will allow you to wield a great deal of influence over the decisions of buyers.

As a rule, make sure your offer (which includes you, remember) engages at least three of the human drives. Make a deliberate attempt to do so. Write your brochures and the copy on your website with these drives in mind.

Take the time in all your interactions to listen to and gain a better understanding of where the buyer is coming from. See if you can detect the buyer's drive to acquire when it arises. Be on the lookout for the desire to defend. And try to bond with the buyer. The subconscious power of the human drives is staggering, and your ability to influence a buyer to commit to backing your idea, buying your product or engaging with your cause will come down to your ability to tap in to his or her individual expressions of these drives.

EASY TO JUSTIFY

Say you are in the market for a new car. Let's assume for a moment that you like sports cars but your budget prevents you from getting an exotic high-performance model. After weeks of shopping, years of dreaming and researching, you find yourself in a dealership that has just acquired a brand-new, extremely well-priced sports coupé. This is a beautiful car. It has a 3.8 liter engine, goes from 0 to 60 miles per hour in around six seconds and looks phenomenal. Brand new, drive away, you can get it for only $50,000. Why? Because it is a Hyundai.

Also on the lot is a pre-owned BMW 330 ci (convertible) with 30,000 miles on the clock. The car still looks pretty good, but it has clearly done some driving. It is neither as fast nor as contemporary as either the newer models of the same BMW or the Hyundai coupé we just talked about.

The Hyundai comes with a lifetime drive-train warranty, five years of free servicing and basically anything else you would ever need to feel sure about the quality of this car. The BMW, on the other hand, has a couple of months left on its original four-year warranty, and you know servicing will be expensive and inevitable.

Which car do you buy?

How you answer this question says a lot about you, how you express your drive to acquire and the brands that you feel support your sense of identity. Let's assume you buy the BMW. Why? Because it is a trusted brand and the Europeans are better known for quality than the Koreans . . .

Really? Did you know that in 2009 a Hyundai model was rated on the J. D. Power Rankings for Initial Quality Study as the fourth-best quality car? Meanwhile, BMW's highest placing was 16th. Hyundai is so confident in the quality of its car that it will fix it and service it for you for free.

166

You might come up with some counter-arguments, such as the BMW would be safer, and that the J. D. Power Rankings are based on buyer opinions and therefore the expectations for the Hyundai would always be lower—and that is probably right. But this does not negate the fact that the Hyundai, as a newer model, is four years ahead of the BMW in the technology stakes.

You see, you will make up all sorts of specifications and features to back up your decision when really you bought the BMW because it sounds better to tell people you drive a Beamer than it does to say you drive a Hyundai. In other words, it is all about brand, and your drive to acquire is manifested in owning and driving brands that you believe give you a higher social standing than those around you.

So what does this mean for you, the seller? A lot! You can't just appeal to the four drives. You need to deliver, on a plate, the justifications that the buyer needs to support his or her emotional decision.

Be it J. D. Power Rankings, or the fact the BMW is made in Germany, or some other specification or point of detail that helps the buyer to support publicly the reasons for choosing you and your offer, you need "stuff" to support his or her story. You need to be easy to justify.

This is what I call "the code"—the language people use to justify their decisions within the tribes they bond with. We can't say, "I bought a BMW because it will make me feel more powerful and successful than my next-door neighbor." We have to be able to say we bought the BMW because it has such a "phenomenal safety record."

The funny thing about the code is that it extends to what is called the social contract as well. Even if our

167

neighbor knows all the information I gave above about Hyundai versus BMW, he or she will probably not give voice to it. Why? Because that, too, is not the done thing. The neighbor will be adhering to his or her part of the code. And the code is the first of two key strategies to being easy to justify.

The second is metrics. You need to speak the language of the buyer, and you need to offer the buyer metrics to support his or her decision. In the case of the BMW, you don't just want to be able to justify your decision by saying, "It was made in Germany, so it must be safe." It is much better if you can quote how the BMW 3 Series has been rated in the top ten best cars in the world on 18 different occasions, or in the case of the Hyundai that it has a five-star safety rating for front and side impact, and the BMW has a four-star rating for the front and five for the side. These are both metrics, and both help buyers to make engaging with you easy to justify.

The Code

If you thought the nuances of deciding which car to buy were complicated, wait until your buyer works for a company. Most of the time, the idea you have and are trying to turn into results will require that you engage people who themselves will need to engage someone around them to support their decision to engage with you. In other words, as we have already seen, there is always another buyer, to whom the buyer needs to justify his or her decision. A buyer may have engaged you as a consultant because he or she liked you, but this has to be expressed to his or her boss as being based on your track record and the recommendations that came from other, similar businesses.

Your job as the seller is to make it as easy as possible for as many buyers as possible to justify their purchase to themselves and to their bosses. And you do this by understanding their code and packaging your proposition in a manner that appeals to that code. This is different from "Easy to Support," which was about finding evidence to support a broader market need, such as the need for executive coaching or the need for more sustainable business practices. Being easy to justify is offering your buyer the "stuff" he or she needs to mask his or her deep personal motivation for buying, which is not always in the best interest of the buyer's company. In other words, it allows the buyer to perpetuate the myth that he or she is acting in the organization's best interest. Bullshit? Yes! Effective? Very!

Allow me to explain better what the code is.

I used to have a great client. I say used to, because I no longer do business with that client. My relationship was with one of the most senior executives at what is one of the biggest professional-service firms in the world. This guy had travelled the world, made plenty of money and in my opinion was about as nice and as centered a man as I'd ever met. In some ways, I aspired to be like him.

And then, out of nowhere, he was gone. His email came back with the automated response that he had left the company. He no longer answered any of his phones, and when I finally got chatting to the CEO he was so cagey about what had happened that I could only assume he had been fired for some very unethical behavior. My retainer was not extended, as I had no one to work with until his replacement had been found. Yet I did not really care about the lost business. I was desperate to know what had happened to this guy, partly because I liked him so much (drive to bond) and also because I just had to know (drive to comprehend).

It sat at the back of my mind for a good six months, when out of nowhere I got a call from my old client. As it turned out, he had basically had a mental breakdown. He was so unhappy and so unfulfilled in his work that it had almost destroyed him. He was, in his own words, deeply depressed. Without sounding flippant, I have to admit I was both very surprised and extremely curious all at the same time. We agreed to have lunch.

So, over lunch I mentioned that I had been hearing about this a lot more lately, and my friend responded by saying that he was starting a new business working with executives on this very issue, and that some of his preliminary research indicated that more than half of all senior managers exhibit some signs of depression. He was emphatic that his anecdotal experience—and he had plenty—supported this notion.

I asked, "Surely something would have to be getting done about this, if it is as widespread as you say?"

He responded, "Something is being done about it. It is called executive coaching."

Coaching has been one of the fastest-growing professional services for executives over the last decades. Thousands of new businesses have sprung up, and surveys abound suggesting that more than three-quarters of all executives have had some form of mentoring and coaching.

And, according to my friend, it is because executives are all so depressed! Okay, I am being a little too dramatic here, but I want you to think about the possibility that this is at least partly true, that many of the people we look up to may in fact be deeply unfulfilled. And now I want you to ask yourself the question why, assuming this is true, does it not get talked about? The answer is that it is quite simply not appropriate, or should I say not acceptable, to admit your flaws in the cut-throat world of business and government. Saying, "I am depressed," could be a career-limiting move. And that is why we never book "counseling" for our people; we always book "coaching." It is also why book titles are generally "positive." It is called the train test. If someone was to see you reading your book on a train, would you be tempted to cover it with a brown paper bag?

So, if you are selling counseling to businesses, as my friend wanted to, you certainly would not call it this. You would call it "executive coaching." Consider these other examples. Instead of teaching new graduates to manage-up, we teach them reputation management. Instead of telling people they are dreadful and that we want them to leave, we put them through performance management. Behind closed doors, we say we are performance managing them out of the business. We don't talk about weaknesses, we talk about areas for improvement. These are all instances of "code."

171

The code is the reason we don't say to people that we give money to charity because it makes us feel less guilty about the indulgent lifestyle we live, while a third of the world's population lives in absolute and devastating poverty. We say our charitable giving is "for a good cause" and we feel generous for what is usually a relatively small donation.

What I am trying to say is that in the market there is a code. And you need to adhere to the code if you want to make your proposition easy to justify. By using the code, you make it easier for the buyer to support his or her decision to engage with you should it ever come into question.

You don't ignore the need that sits behind the communicated need, but you package what you are offering in a way that matches the external market language of the buyer, not the internal dialogue and unconscious language of the buyer. You don't package your cost-cutting strategy as "firing a whole lot of people and putting them out of work"; you package it as "business process optimization" or "creating leaner organizations." You don't package the property you sell as "you will finally prove to your father that you made it"; you package it as "you work hard and deserve to live in a nice home." In short, you adhere to the code.

A question worth exploring here is why do so many industries have such complex codes? In many cases, you can trace it back to the drives. Sometimes, the complexity of the code allows prospective buyers to raise the barriers of entry into their market (drive to defend). Sometimes, it gives them a sense of belonging to an exclusive group (drive to bond). Other times, the code itself actually makes it easier to understand the relevant concepts from within that community (drive to comprehend), and other

172

times still it is a sign of having attained an elite status (drive to acquire).

One of the reasons that buyers love having a code is not just to justify why they buy but also to justify why they do not. The code will be used against you in the Positioning and Influence phases. The buyer will use it as a way of discriminating against you and what you are selling. If you don't know the code, you can't play our game.

Do your research. Read as many industry publications as you can and brush up on your code. Knowing what buyers are allowed to spend money on, and how they have to phrase that internally, is a very important concept.

In fact, I personally think it is rude not to get on their wavelength. If you are going to ask people to exchange something they value with you, the very least you can do is make an effort to understand their world. Recently, I was approached by an association of universities in Canada about presenting and they asked me to send them some information about what I speak on. Rather than send them a standard, generic flyer listing my key topics, I instead spent the next 60 minutes researching the state of Canadian universities and specifically their effectiveness at partnering with private enterprise and commercializing their research.

I then sent a long email to the agent, who responded with a thank you but suggested that I had completely missed the brief—which, on reflection, I had. He sent my email through nonetheless because of the effort I had gone to and the client came back with, "This is exactly what we want." The association had not known how to ask for it, or if someone who was outside its industry

173

would be able to offer that insight. Because I used its language and identified its industry trends and challenges, I had adhered to the code and was able to get it to engage.

Now, the real lesson here is not that I had ensured my offer matched their market need. That was the point of "Easy to Support" back in the section on positioning. What we need to understand here are the personal motivations of the individual buyer. Ask yourself, is it risky booking a speaker you have previously never heard of for your major annual convention? What is the risk? That they suck! And why is that bad at a personal level? Because everyone will hold you responsible, which will have a negative impact on your credibility, affect your "bond" with your peers and generally make you look and feel stupid.

By using the code, I was able to nullify many of these concerns, because I was able to make it clear I was not an idiot. With the same lengthy email, I included four testimonials from extremely high-profile companies (more on that soon) and a video link of me speaking at dozens of major conferences. So now my buyer was able to say to her buyers, "He has done this before. He looked good on video and he clearly understands our industry." Tick, tick, tick. I had removed most of the personal risk.

Let me share with you a commercial example and then a charitable example to drive the point home.

What is the difference between Coke Zero and Diet Coke? Or between Pepsi Max and Diet Pepsi? As it turns out, not a lot. It is simply in the sweetener that is used to replace the sugar in the regular versions of the mother brands.

174

So why the two different products that are so similar? Different buyers, that's why! Men don't drink diet products; women do. Pepsi Max, and all its advertising around extreme sports, is an attempt to attract more health-conscious men who would not want to be seen drinking diet anything. You see, with the health trend that has helped catapult companies such as Subway and 24 Hour Fitness to massive success and spawned more dietary-supplements companies than people in China, men were becoming as health conscious as women. However, drinking diet products was not the "thing to do." Put differently, the "diet" proposition threatened men's personal identity and their drive to bond.

The success of Coke Zero is evidence of how powerful knowing the code, and the drives of the buyer, can be. Coke Zero was Coca-Cola's biggest product launch in 22 years. A hallmark of the campaign was the viral rumor that spread suggesting that executives were so angry about the similarity of taste between regular Coke and Coke Zero that they were considering suing their co-workers for "taste infringement."

Due to the attempt to attract young males, the edginess of the various campaigns attracted a certain amount of criticism, but this boldness only further cemented the relevance of the Coke Zero brand in the minds of the male market it was seeking. And the evidence is in the result. There were 350 sparkling-soda-product launches between 2001 and 2008, and only six have managed to get a market share of above one percent. Coke Zero is one of them—all because of code. Sure money helps, but New Coke had plenty of money behind it and look how that turned out.

175

One of the major trends I have seen in my life is that of getting behind much more narrow causes and charities as opposed to simply giving to your church or supporting the Salvation Army or the Red Cross.

The competition for donor money is fierce, and charities employ some very powerful tools of influence to get people to buy. One of these is most certainly code. The offering of a charity is heavily coded in order to find the intersection between its offering and what the donor is really looking for. Remember here that what the donor is looking for and what the donor says he or she is looking for might be very different things.

The psychology of charity has been discussed at great length in other places. At the risk of oversimplifying, there are three reasonable explanations for why people donate to charity:

1. They are just good people who are committed to making a difference.
2. They want to make themselves feel that they are making a difference in order to assuage their guilt so they can sleep at night.
3. They want to show the rest of the world how good and generous they are.

These last two points may seem a little cynical at first, and you are free to believe that everyone donates because it is the right thing to do. However, you may be interested to know that the act of giving stimulates the same part of the brain that responds to food and sex. In an experiment at the National Institutes of Health, again involving brain scans, the participants were given a sum of money and the choice to either donate it to a charity or keep it for themselves. When the participant chose an act of generosity and gave the money to a charity, it stimulated the primitive part of the brain that is hard-wired to pleasure. In other words, acts of kindness may be no more than the basic human disposition to do things that are pleasurable. Better than sex, drugs and rock 'n' roll, wouldn't you say? Well, maybe not all the time.

Consider World Vision and the poignant ads it runs about starving children in the Third World. It doesn't run ads that say you should feel ashamed at the abundance you have and you should give more money. It runs ads that talk about the plight of children, use high-impact imagery and make simple comparisons such as for $1 a day you could save a child from starvation. This does make you feel a little guilty about your abundance, but without ever saying it explicitly. And it makes you feel some compassion as your mirror neurons are firing in empathy for the plight of these children. Then, whether it be your guilt or your humanity or even your desire for a greater sense of personal well-being, you will call the number and sponsor a child.

In a strange twist, World Vision needs to make you realize that giving the money will make you feel good and at the same time suppress the drive to defend that makes you want to keep the money in fear that you will lose your status and wealth if you don't protect your finances.

The code in charity—the publicly tolerable and acceptable offering—is that you are "making a difference." So

177

charities position themselves publicly as making a difference. They position the problem they are solving for the child instead of the problem they are solving for the buyer, knowing full well that this will make you very aware of the need you have to feel better, to do the right thing and to help humanity. They tap in to your drive to acquire (connected to your sense of well-being) and your drive to bond (reflected in your care and love for humanity). The more they humanize the faces on the TV, give them names, tell you about their lives, the more it appeals to your drive to bond.

Where I believe they get really smart is in showing you specifically what your donation will buy. I have even seen ads that show you three levels of donation. $10 will buy school books for a year; $20 will feed them for a week; and $100 will give them clean water for a year. How could you not give the $100, right?

And this last reference is a perfect example of how to use metrics and numbers to support your offer. If you can allow buyers to justify their behavior by giving them measurable ways to support their decision, you are a long way to becoming easy to justify.

Metrics

Metrics are a sore point for many of us on our journey to taking our ideas and turning them into reality. We really do believe that what we do is positive for the buyer, and we really want someone to engage with us. The problem is, what we do may not be able to be measured. Well, I hate to say it, but if you can't measure it, it is much harder

178

to sell. And remember that measure means show how it adds value in a way that is acceptable for the code.

To say that your HR consultancy will make people happier at work is one thing. Having survey data to support that notion may be useful too. But in reality, unless you can show how having happy workers increases productivity and therefore profitability, selling happiness is outside of the code. Metrics can be hard to define. Or, if you are like me, from time to time you miss the metric altogether and make your offer with evidence of things the buyer does not really care about.

At least, this is what I did once (or perhaps I should say more than once). I am often asked to present at large public events, some of which attract literally thousands of people. I remember one of the first times I spoke at one of these, it was in Toronto, Canada. I was the first speaker on the program and felt it was an honor to be presenting along with the other people on the card. These included the 20-time world chess champion Gary Kasparov, the recent eight-gold-medal-winning athlete Michael Phelps and the multi-award-winning journalist Barbara Walters.

I did my talk and thought it went well, yet I have never been invited back. I could not believe it. The audience loved it, but the client did not. You see, I was used to speaking almost exclusively to business audiences dealing with major challenges around staff retention or a lack of innovation in the business. My ability to deal with these issues directly and offer cost-effective, proven strategies was considered highly valuable. The audience surveys even said so. To this new client, the event promoter, the ideas themselves mattered not one bit. Nothing mattered unless it led to people buying more tickets. This is not a bad thing, it is how his business model worked, and I was negligent not to realize this.

I had met the market need—engaged an audience—but not my buyer's need for more ticket sales. In many ways, I actually missed the market altogether by thinking it was about the audience. My market is the event operator in this instance, and this promoter owned his business. I failed to meet his drive to acquire.

My guess is that the post-seminar survey of the audience asked two very telling questions. Which speakers did you enjoy the most? Which speakers did you come to see? I know I nailed the first question, with rave reviews, but when it came to the second I failed miserably. Of the thousands in attendance, I reckon less than a hundred stated that I was the speaker they came to see. My brand just did not have that much pulling power for this broad audience.

The more I thought about it, the more I understood. If I was a promoter, one of the keys to building a successful business was not to book speakers who perhaps I liked, or who were good speakers, but to book people who would sell tickets. It is, after all, about the audience and what makes them buy. What I had failed to realize is that what the promoter needed, and the metric by which he would judge my effectiveness, was not based on how many people liked me but on how many people bought tickets because of me. My buyer's metric was not audience engagement, it was not audience satisfaction, it was tickets sold. And, fair enough, I was not on the card next year, even though one or two of the other speakers there that day were.

As we said right up front, markets have metrics by which buyers determine the value of your offering. What metrics does your buyer value? And how can you measure and communicate your ability to hit those metrics?

The key to knowing the metrics is to know:

- The business model.
- The reporting systems of your buyer.

The business model is quite simple: Where and how do they make money? The reporting systems are, what does your buyer get judged on by his or her buyers? How is he or she evaluated?

Now, if you can package your offer to show evidence of how you can actually measure and prove your ability to add value in the way the buyer needs, you will find your powers of influence expanded exponentially.

10

THE SELLER

AS THE SELLER, you need to make the buyer believe you and like you. It has to be both. If a buyer believes you but does not like you, he or she will find someone else to work with. The buyer can like you but not believe you, at which point he or she definitely won't work with you. So, obviously, your seller-related strategies are to be:

- Easy to believe.
- Easy to like.

EASY TO BELIEVE

To say you are easy to believe is the same as saying the buyer trusts you. I have a formula for trust that I have borrowed and tweaked from my friend Peter Fuda (whom I mentioned earlier for his work on transformational change), which you might find useful.

$$\text{TRUST} = \frac{\text{CREDIBILITY} + \text{AUTHENTICITY}}{\text{SELF-INTEREST}}$$

Trust formula

Trust equals credibility plus authenticity divided by self-interest. So, if you are the seller and I believe you are credible (competent and able to do what you say) and authentic (genuine and willing to do what you say), then my level of trust in you is building. That trust, however, is reduced by how much I think you have to gain from the interaction. If the benefits seem mainly in your favor, the natural skepticism we all have will kick in and I will trust you less. If the exchange does not seem to be all about you getting what you want, then my level of trust in you will be higher.

In 1982, Barry J. Marshall and Robin Warren made a claim based on their research that stomach ulcers were caused by bacteria. This claim flew in the face of much of what the medical establishment knew and believed about ulcers and as such was met with a healthy skepticism that has also been called outright rejection and ridicule.

Now, I know it was a pretty bold claim, but what if they had been researchers at Harvard instead of the University of Western Australia? Working in a very small city, one of the most isolated in the world, despite its proven prowess in research (in Australia at least), does not bring with it the credibility that would come with being a researcher at

183

Harvard or Princeton or some other globally respected institution.

After a series of ineffective experiments on piglets, Marshall was so exasperated that he drank a mixture of the very bacteria he was claiming created ulcers just to prove his point. Needless to say, he was right, and the paper he and Warren went on to publish in the *Medical Journal of Australia* become one of the journal's most commonly cited. Marshall and Warren were awarded the Nobel Prize for Medicine in 2005 as a result. As a Nobel Prize winner, you can be sure Marshall no longer has to do crazy things such as drink his bacterial poison to prove his point. Why? Because a Nobel Prize gives him credibility.

Credibility is why professionals such as doctors, dentists and lawyers display their framed diplomas on their office walls. It is why lobbyists, corporate executives and dealmakers almost always have a "trophy wall" in their office with pictures of them with the great and near-great. It is credibility by association, in many cases. It is why estate agents drive cars they can barely afford. They want you to feel you are in the presence of success.

In order to have any influence over another human being, that human being needs to consider you credible. If that person considers you credible, he or she believes you can do what you say. That does not mean he or she believes you will. In order for the person to believe you will do it, he or she must think you are being authentic.

184

Another way of saying this is that the person in question must feel you are a person of integrity—that you will deliver on your promises.

Let me detail here seven things that will enhance your ability to convince the buyer of your credibility and authenticity:

1. Passion and persistence.
2. Appearance.
3. Referrals.
4. Testimonials.
5. Guarantees.
6. Price.
7. Pitch less, pull more.

Passion and Persistence

At this point, I want to share with you something that will blow your mind. And it is based on the work of the now-famous psychologist Daniel Gilbert, the author of *Stumbling on Happiness*. Long before he wrote that book, he penned a phenomenal essay for the *Journal of Personality and Social Psychology* that laid out evidence that merely hearing or reading a statement inescapably meant believing it.

At first, this makes no sense, right? People don't believe everything they hear and read! Well, as it turns out, they do, at least for a short while. In order to understand something, you must believe it. I could bore you with the science but would rather not waste your time. The reason we don't accept everything is that very quickly after understanding and believing something we set out to test it and decide whether we will continue to believe it. We retroactively discredit or "unbelieve" it.

185

Perhaps most powerful for you as a seller is that the more passionately you communicate something, the more intensely the buyer believes it before beginning to wonder if it is really true. At the most intense end of the scale, the buyer never questions the initial belief but clings to it forever after.

In every other kind of life encounter, the first impression—the first belief, positive or negative, that someone has about something or someone else—is the strongest. Human beings have always known this to be true, which is why your mum wanted you to look nice on your first day of school and your dad told you to shine your shoes before your first job interview. Thanks to Daniel Gilbert and other recent research, we finally know why it is true at a neuronal level.

The stronger the emotional intensity during comprehension, the more likely the buyer is to remember the episode. Think about yourself. Have you ever had an intense emotional experience in your life? Of course you have. Can you forget it? No. Especially the embarrassing ones. They are so deeply ingrained in your memory that it seems as if they will never be forgotten.

Passion drives the memory of your offer deep into the mind of the buyer. Passion sells.

The other great thing is that the more times you repeat the assertion, the more likely someone is to believe it. Strangely, one person's repeated assertion is thought to be 90 percent as powerful as three different people making that assertion. Wow! Just by repeating yourself, you are increasing the likelihood of being believed. This is because the other way of implanting an enduring memory

186

is to use repetition. Passion generates emotional intensity, which ingrains the experience deeply. Persistence repeats the experience and, over time, ingrains it in much the same way.

Think on this for a minute. This is why people say you need to get your foot in the door. Or you may have even said it yourself: "If only I could explain my idea, the buyer would be interested." This is psychologically true. So the key to becoming easy to believe is actually about being easy to keep believing. The passion with which you lay the initial belief (through understanding) helps it "stick" in the buyer's mind. And the repetition not only helps to make it stick but also interrupts the "unbelieving" process that is unconsciously taking place in the mind of the buyer.

Finally, if you want to be easy to believe, you had better believe it yourself. If you believe it yourself, there is a much greater chance that you will communicate it with passion and that you will not take no for an answer, per-sisting in spite of initial rejection until the buyer finally gets it. Perhaps standing in front of the mirror and saying nice things to yourself is in fact a useful activity. It is if it helps you believe in the offer you are trying to sell.

However, beyond passion and simple repetition, there are other powerful ways you can encourage the buyer to keep believing you. The following strategies are targeted at nullifying the retroactive process of "unbelieving" you.

Appearance

I often argue with one of my colleagues about the perils of wearing odd socks and ones that don't go with the pants he is wearing. He says that is way too conformist, and that his disregard for the "rules" is a statement of his quirky view of the world.

Socks sound trivial, I know, but when you realize that he is the Chief Creative Officer and shareholder in a company I started and majority own, you start to realize why I have an opinion. My contention is that personal dress is enough to make someone discriminate against him when deciding whether or not to do business with us. Whether the buyer distrusts people who don't dress formally or sees it as a lack of attention to detail, I just don't think we should provide a potential client with a superficial way to squeeze us off his or her mental menu—or, worse, keep us firmly positioned in there for all the wrong reasons.

The first question a buyer might raise about your credibility and authenticity is based on how you present yourself. What are you wearing, how do you speak and how do you conduct yourself? What scares me most about this is that it happens so quickly and so automatically that the buyer will not even realize he or she is doing it. Have you ever had a bug land on your arm and without even thinking you have jumped three feet in the air, swung your other hand around and completely annihilated this tiny little creature? This is due to your adaptive unconsciousness, and it is at work 24/7/365 in your and your buyer's mind.

You must not underestimate the power of these impressions. In a study at Princeton, again using MRI machines, researchers were able to show that we make judgments about people's trustworthiness in 100 milliseconds, which is the time it takes your amygdala to respond to visual stimuli, even though we have not had time to consciously process what we are looking at. When asked about how much or how little they trusted a face, the subjects' amygdalae could be used to accurately predict their answers, as the amygdalae had made up their minds before the subjects' conscious minds had swung into action. Remember the adaptive unconscious?

Because we are so quick to make judgments based on visual stimuli, the way you present yourself and how in tune that is with the identity of the buyer could be the difference between engaging that buyer and not. Studies have shown that even when it comes to voting, 70 percent of people still vote along the same lines as their first unconscious impression after seeing many debates and a whole lot of campaigning. PLAY . . . THE . . . GAME!

The adaptive unconscious is characterized by its speed, the effortlessness with which we employ it and its complete inflexibility. Because it happens by itself, we have little influence over the snap judgments we make as a result of it. If you have ever been in a job interview, you can be pretty sure the decision about whether or not to hire you was made within minutes, if not seconds, of you entering the room.

The same is true of the impression you make on the buyer. This I think you already know, and its application to the concept of credibility is clear. What is more fascinating and eye-opening is how a buyer will make the very same snap judgments about your integrity. What you wear and how you speak will have an impact on whether they believe you will deliver on your promises. You may be interested to know that the presence of a beard will generally make a buyer distrust you. Crazy, huh?

189

Well, if you really want to get crazy, expand your understanding of the senses we use to make these judgments. They are sight, sound, smell, touch and taste. (Okay, taste only comes into play depending on what you are selling, but you know what I mean.) Granted, it is now believed we have ten senses, including balance, acceleration, kinaesthesia, and others, but the point I want to make is that we pick up a lot from the traditional five senses.

Can buyers "smell" our intention to rip them off? Do they pick up subtle cues from our facial expressions about when we are faking it? There is a growing body of evidence that suggests they indeed can. Have you ever had a conversation with someone whom you knew was full of crap? The answer will surely be yes. But how did you know? You just did. (Again, this is a book in itself.) Here is what I suggest you do about this:

- Get clear about your intention. What do you intend to have the buyer do?
- Why? If your answer is purely selfish, you need to check in again and find a reason for the buyer to engage that is good for both the buyer and you, and keep that at the front of your mind.
- Ask yourself what sort of person this buyer would want to engage with.
- How would that person dress, speak and generally "show up?"
- How close is that to you?
- Get as close as you can to that image, but never so much that you feel out of your league. If you lose confidence, buyers will smell it. They will just know!

This is a fine balance. I am basically saying that you shouldn't fake it, because an attempt to build false credibility will be sensed as a lack of authenticity. Remember, trust is about both. Yet I am saying you should push the edges of your comfort zone. Appearance and the way you come across matters, and you should put some thought into making it work for you.

Referrals

When Jamie Foxx won the Oscar for his role in *Ray*, he received a call from Denzel Washington to congratulate him. Foxx had on more than one occasion made it clear that Denzel was his acting idol, so needless to say he was taken aback to receive Denzel's kind words.

The story goes that Foxx joked that Denzel Washington was not meant to be calling him, implying that he was not worthy to be receiving such a call. Denzel's response was, "Kings talk to kings."

If your buyer is powerful, connected and hard to get to, there is probably only one kind of person he will listen to—and that is another king. Now, put aside the male notion of kings, because kings talk to queens and queens talk to queens, and so on. It is a metaphor, you maniac, so insert whatever sex you want.

The best way to get in front of a buyer, and for that buyer to trust you quickly, is for you to be referred to that person by someone he or she already knows, likes and trusts. And herein lies the power of your network. Influence is greatly enhanced if you leverage the existing people you know, who already trust you. This will grant you

191

instant credibility, implied authenticity and acceptance of your self-interest.

One of the great challenges of your personal network is that it is very difficult to know who your friends know. At times, it is difficult to remember who you know. I was reading recently that on average we have about 165 people we could call who would know who we are. Call them friends, acquaintances, whatever. There is a pre-earned level of trust within that group. Now, imagine you know the 165 people whom they each know. Just in that network, barely one degree of separation from you, is a potential network of 27,225 people. That is, 27,225 people who would believe you, based on the recommendation of someone they already trusted. Surely some of them will be buyers.

You have all heard the concept of six degrees of separation. That is, everyone on earth is connected to us to within six degrees of relationship separation. Your friends are one degree away. Their friends, that are not your friends, are the second degree, and on it goes. The only problem with six being the magic number is that it is based on a very rough experiment done by Stanley Milgram in 1967 using phone books. More recent research at Columbia suggests the correct number is between five and seven, and yet others at the Massachusetts Institute of Technology suggest that it is potentially less than five. If this is true, you can reach any buyer, anywhere, in fewer than six degrees of separation.

So how do you do it? Technology! Social-networking sites such as LinkedIn and Facebook allow you to stay connected with your friends and colleagues like never before—although Facebook is probably not a great medium for selling. Very few of the buyers I interact with on a daily basis are even on Facebook, and the ones that are use it for personal reasons and would rather not be sold to through this website. LinkedIn, on the other hand, is positioned as a professional network, and people expect to conduct commercial interactions on it. If you are not aware of LinkedIn, go and check it out. It is very simple to use and you can be up and running and connecting to your colleagues in a matter of minutes.

Imagine the power of having a profile of everyone you know searchable at your fingertips, but that when you searched you could also find their contacts and their contacts' contacts. And that the system would send back to you the shortest possible routes for connecting to the buyers you want to reach.

I just took a quick look at my LinkedIn, and I have an unimpressive 120 contacts. (Some of my friends have hundreds.) And yet through my 120 contacts I have a searchable network of over 1,200,000 professionals.

You get the point. The quickest way to get in front of and influence a buyer through trust is to be referred by someone the buyer already trusts and respects. Whether you use technology to manage those relationships or not is beside the point. It helps to be referred!

Testimonials

Patricia Fripp is a great professional speaker. When she is asked to send information about her work to prospective clients, she includes pages and pages of testimonials from respected clients with powerful brands saying how wonderful she is. A testimonial from a CEO whom people recognize about the quality of your work brings an instant credibility to what you do. Four pages of them is even better. Or, as she would say, "How could that many people be wrong?"

If all these other people are willing to declare to the world that you can be trusted, that you are both credible and have integrity, then you must have something going for you. The people offering the testimonials are putting their professional reputations on the line in supporting you, so they must be confident that you are not going to let them down. This is no different from the people you see vouching for beauty products or weight-loss strategies on TV.

The power of a testimonial is generally dictated by the power of the brand giving it. This is known as credibility by association. Kings talk to kings, yes, but princes want to hang out with kings even more. You see, the one thing better than being given a testimonial from a peer of the buyer is to be given a testimonial from someone the buyer aspires to emulate.

Having a CEO offer you a testimonial or getting it from a recognized brand powerhouse is worth 20 testimonials from people and brands with which the buyer does not identify himself or herself. I will talk more about this concept of identity under "Easy to Like," and this will become even clearer when we do.

Ask yourself: if you were hiring a technical IT person and one had three years' experience at Google and the other had three years' experience at a company you had never heard of, who would you instantly assume had the most cred? The Google person, no doubt! What powerful brands are you already affiliated with that you could use to enhance your credibility just by association?

But testimonials are about more than having people say nice things about you, or enhancing your credibility through association. They really do suggest that you have a track record of doing what you say, that you have some integrity. This, you will come to realize, will be key not just here but when you attempt to reinvent yourself too.

At this point, we should return to your idea itself. It is quite possible that you have never done what you are now trying to sell. You have done other things, but not this. It is not the end of the world. If you have a track record of having delivered in the past, the buyer has good reason to assume that you can continue to do this.

A way of taking the concept of a testimonial further is to develop full-blown case studies, including measurable results and reports of the impact you have made in this and other areas. If you have already built an orphanage in Thailand, there is no reason why a donor won't believe you can build one in Vietnam too.

Someone else saying you are good is always better than you saying you are good.

Guarantees

In a very real way, the whole "Easy to Believe" strategy is about risk mitigation, which itself appeals to the drive to defend. As such, anything you can do to remove the risk of engaging you will make it more likely for the buyer to believe you.

195

Money-back guarantees, service guarantees and the like make it very difficult for the buyer, or those to whom the buyer reports, to question whether or not your offer is too risky. If the buyer has the option of getting his or her money back any time, for any reason, say, then what do they have to lose? Time and energy, of course, but at least you have removed the monetary risk.

I mentioned Hyundai earlier. When Hyundai offers a lifetime guarantee on its engines, it is hard to argue with the company's claims about quality. When it offers to service your car for free as well, it is basically saying that it is so confident that nothing will ever go wrong with this car that it will pay for it if it does. And for an unbelievably pioneering strategy, check out what it did during the plummeting sales of cars in the global financial crisis. In addition to the amazing warranties it offered in support of its quality claims, it also pioneered the Hyundai Assurance program, which would allow its customers to return their new car to the dealer without penalty if they were to lose their job as a result of the recession within the first year of owning the vehicle. Talk about removing the risk of the potential loss of the buyer in a transaction.

This appeals directly to the drive to defend, ensuring that the buyer will not be left high and dry with a new-car debt and no job.

Oh, and did it work? When some automakers' sales were down as much as 30 percent from the year prior, Hyundai was up three percent. The company was bang on trend. Its "good value" brand was perfectly positioned, and all its sales reps needed to do to influence buyers was remind them of the tremendous value it offered, the quality ratings

196

we have mentioned and the amazing guarantee that if they lost their jobs, Hyundai had their backs. And if you want to know that it works, Hyundai's market share is now more than 3 times what it was 10 years ago. In the world of automotive sales this is unparalleled over the same period.

I once facilitated a sales-and-marketing strategy day for one of the biggest distributors of business hardware in the world. It sells servers, and lots of them, among other things. After much discussion and brainstorming, it was decided by the team that the biggest barrier to making a sale in the current environment was the buyers' fears that they would spend all this money and the server would not be as fast, capable or reliable as it was meant to be. So, in a very bold move, this company decided to instigate a money-back, fully serviced removal of a server if for any reason the client decided within nine months that the product was not up to standard. When you think about the fact that many buyers treat servers as commodities (as in, they are all the same so just go for the cheapest price), this is a powerful incentive. It says we believe in our product so strongly, and we are so certain that you will too, that we will, at no cost to you, come and remove it at any stage in the next nine months and give you all the money back that you paid for the hardware.

The truth be told, no buyer would ever take the seller up on this, because of the time and money invested in configuring a new server to the company's IT infrastructure, but it made a powerful statement, and in addition to making its offer more believable it also gave the buyer the necessary code to justify his or her decision to the necessary people.

Needless to say, the seller's legal department had a fit, but screw legal. This is about making the sale, and on too many occasions the paranoia of legal departments kills ideas that are good for the business. No promises come without risks, but if the product is as good as you are saying, you should be prepared to put your money where your mouth is, for instant credibility.

Price

There is no question there are some buyers out there who look for the cheapest price. People like me try to deny it, but in many cases the cheapest provider who can tick all the boxes gets the gig. However, there is a growing group of buyers that looks not for the cheapest but for the most valuable. Now, the concept of value is an interesting one, and depends on what market you are trying to serve.

McKinsey & Co. will not be the cheapest consultant you can bring into your business to do strategy but its track record and professionalism may make it the most effective and therefore the best value.

In a different sense, the whole purpose of making a purchase is to acquire something that gives you a sense of well-being. In other words, you want to eat at an expensive restaurant because it is an expensive restaurant. You might be making a statement to yourself: maybe it is your partner's birthday, or maybe you are trying to impress a client.

Wine naturally comes to mind in this respect. In recent times, there has been a general consensus that in markets, such as wine, price is expected to have a correlation with quality. In other words, a wine is expensive because of its

198

quality. However, recent research, based on more than 6000 taste tests, showed that, for normal consumers of wine (trained sommeliers are an exception), the wine was good because it was expensive, and not the other way around. When they did a blind taste test, preventing the drinker from seeing either the label or the price, it turned out that the drinkers generally preferred the cheaper wine. When they did the same experiment but allowing people to see the packaging and know the price, the opposite happened. The researchers concluded that the price itself impacted the perception of quality. The study to which I refer was published as a working paper in April 2008 at www.wine-economics.org.

If you want to encourage someone to buy your services instead of someone else's, then, the fact that you are more expensive may actually work in your favor, not against you. And if you are subtle in the way you pitch it, you can make the buyer feel that paying you a premium is less risky than opting for the other provider who is cheaper and seems more desperate.

This is much easier said than done. When you are trying to get your idea off the ground, you will be pretty desperate just to get that first sale. And, between you and me, sometimes in the early days you should do whatever it takes. Once you have the ball rolling, you will get momentum. You will probably find yourself offering great deals to that client forever, but having him or her vouch for your ability, now that you have delivered on your promise, means you don't need to convince people you can do it. You will have evidence of it. At some stage, though, you need to value what you do. And being too

199

eager to drop your price makes a subliminal statement about quality to the buyer.

Alan Weiss coaches people trying to get into the management-consulting business and wrote a book called *Million Dollar Consulting*. He has a brilliant exercise where he makes you practice quoting your fee in front of the mirror. You need to be able to do it and not laugh. In other words, you need to believe you are worth it.

This may seem like a little thing, but truly believing in what you are selling is half the battle. Believing that your offer can literally transform the life of the buyer will genuinely make it easier for the buyer to believe you.

If you do not have that conviction, if you do not believe in the value enough to charge for it, why should they?

Pitch Less, Pull More

All right, I feel a little guilty about putting this section in, especially before you are on the right-hand side of the buyer's mental menu. I know exactly what it is like to be working furiously to get an idea off the ground. I know how hard it is to make those early sales and how desperate you are for someone, anyone, to buy. The twisted reality is that this very desperation kills your power to influence. One of the great ironies on the journey to making it happen is that when you need buyers, they will be very hard to find, and when finally you don't need them they will be lining up at your door. The latter reality is a great reality indeed, but you have to endure the pain of desperation in order to get there. And yet you will never get there if you appear desperate.

200

Nothing will kill your credibility and heighten a buyer's sense of your self-interest than appearing too eager to sell to him or her. In a way, the art of influence is actually not to sell, despite what I might have implied, but in fact to get the buyer to buy. There is a subtle difference. When you are selling, you come across as trying to shove your offer down the buyer's throat. And the telltale signs of this are:

- You talk way too much.
- You fidget and seem uncomfortable in the meeting.
- You don't seem to be listening to what the buyer is saying.
- You answer questions with pre-authored answers, even if they do not address the real question.
- You appear frustrated and defensive when the buyer asks you for evidence to back up your claims.
- You keep trying to convince them after they have committed.
- You say things that suggest you are scared the buyer will renege on his or her commitment.

Stop it! Now, in the early days you will show up anywhere, any time and place where the opportunity for a sale might exist. I get it. I have done it. But don't discredit yourself by trying to pitch to everyone in the room. This is not smart because it creates the wrong buying dynamic. In other words, it creates an interaction between you and the buyer where instead of the buyer trying to ascertain if he or she should buy from you, you are trying to convince the buyer that he or she should.

201

You need to have the confidence in yourself and your idea and believe so deeply in its value that you authentically act as though the buyer should want to buy from you, more than acting as if you want to sell to them.

The problem is that there are no techniques or tools I can give you to make this easier. In fact, the very use of a technique or tool will be harmful to your authenticity.

People know when you are "doing a technique" on them. Tools are for toolboxes, I say.

This is a matter for personal reflection. You can't fake it. Either you have done the work to develop your idea into a compelling offer or you haven't. Either you know you can provide real value to the buyer or you don't. And if you haven't done the work and are not convinced that you can add value, then you need to go right back to Competency 1 and work out what value you can bring and how you might then package and position that offer.

This is partly why I was so adamant in the piece on differentiation that you embrace who you are and where you come from. It is indeed the only area in which you have any real credibility.

I will give you these pointers, though:

- Talk less, listen more.
- Ask a truck load of questions, especially directed questions such as, "How can you see your business solving problem X?" that elicit the pain points we talked about earlier and also let the buyer come to the conclusion himself or herself that he or she needs what you have.

202

- Study the buyer's world, his or her company, industry and role, before meeting with that person.
- Where possible, let the moment of clarity come from the buyer's mouth, and not yours, and then of course gently remind the buyer that what he or she has just decided he or she needs is what you are in the business of doing.

A buyer is much more likely to believe you if it is indeed he or she who came to the conclusion to engage you without you having to hammer it home.

EASY TO LIKE

It was my first big corporate meeting. The target client, Coles Myer, was the most powerful retailer in Australia. It had 165,000 staff and was the ultimate target for my work with managers on understanding Generation Y and how to position an employer brand to attract the best Gen Y talent.

I arrived for a meeting in Coles Myer's Melbourne headquarters. I had flown down especially, and at the time the airfare was a big dent in my weekly expenditures. The senior executive I had arranged to meet had completely forgotten about our meeting and so sent one of her staff to see me instead.

Being the cocky little brat that I was (or perhaps still am!), I refused to meet with the underling and told (not

203

asked) her to pass the message back to the executive that the least she could do after agreeing to the meeting and making me fly down especially was to give me ten minutes of her time.

Oddly enough, she agreed . . . and a good thing, too— the only other potential response, given the strong force of my statement, was to ask security to escort me off the premises.

As I sat in the executive's office, she rocked back in her chair and in the most condescending way imaginable said, "So, young man, what is it you think you can do for us?"

I explained that I could help them attract better staff to their supermarket branches through effective advertising and campaigning and through the positioning of their employment opportunities. I was doing my best to use her words, and it seemed to soften her disposition ever so slightly.

"So, what could we do better?" she asked next, either putting me to the test to catch me out or maybe, at some level, thinking she might get some free advice.

"Well," my mouth responded before my brain could tell it to shut up, "take that poster on your wall." I motioned to the terribly positioned "cool jobs" poster, the flagship of their Gen Y recruitment campaign. "Cool jobs is a terrible idea for a campaign. Something you need to know about youth culture is that if you have to say it's cool, it's not cool. I mean, come on, who approved that crap?"

Yes . . . you guessed it. She did.

Needless to say, my critique of her work was not appreciated, and the meeting came to an abrupt and unceremonious end. Less than three hours later, I heard from the person who had referred me to the executive that I was being called a "little shit" and that he was never to recommend a person like me again.

As a side note, the "cool jobs" campaign was abandoned and something more authentic followed. Perhaps I did have an impact, but I certainly did not get paid for it.

In the near-decade before the Wesfarmers takeover, I was never asked to meet with or work with that organization. Not because my advice wasn't good, but because I didn't play the political game very well. The buyer did not like me. It was as simple as that. And it was not just because I did not match her or mirror her physiology; it was that my view of the world and hers, and my style of delivering that view, were too far apart for there to be any authentic connection.

When I say that matching and mirroring didn't help in this case, I am not suggesting that this is not a powerful part of influence. It is, and you should learn about it. You have no doubt heard about the importance of mirroring the way the buyer sits, breathes and talks. There is some fascinating work on this area. What I want to do is get behind the technique itself and find out why it works, so we can have a true understanding and mastery of it. We will then be able to apply it at a more powerful level than the physiological—and that is at the psychological.

Why do we respond positively to people who have a similar physiology to our own? What psychological process is going on at this point that makes this attractive? In case you can't guess, the answer will lie in an even deeper understanding of the four drives in our lives (see p. 145).

The problem with going into a meeting and feeling you have to mimic the buyer's body language to get

205

him or her to like you is that it reeks of inauthenticity. If you can find a deeper sense of connection based on who you really are and who he or she really is, you will have a far more trusting relationship from the beginning, and your ability to influence that buyer will be enhanced many times over. I don't believe you should "fake it till you make it." I believe in authenticity. But I also believe you can fast track the connection process by understanding how humans create their sense of identity and how that identity then shapes who they want to engage with.

Think about it this way. We understand the human drive to bond. We know why we have evolved this way and that grouping improves our chances of survival and of our other drives being met. What we don't know is who we are driven to bond with and why. Because we don't like everybody, we don't try to bond with everybody.

If you can understand the psychological process that determines who we like and why, you can start to ensure you represent that for the buyer. And, in order to do that, we are now going beneath the realm of stories and private drives into the deep recesses of the human mind, to the place where we develop and construct our personal identities. This is a powerful place indeed.

The sum total of how your buyer manifests his or her four drives becomes that person's identity. What the buyer has (drive to acquire), who the buyer hangs around with and the groups he or she associates with (drive to bond), what the buyer is prepared to defend (drive to defend) and the way the buyer sees his or her world (drive to comprehend) is who that person is. We are all searching for the answer to the question, "Who am I?" and we find our answer through the aspects above.

However, as you probably can expect, it is not that simple. The drives don't really create the identity; rather, the need for a congruent identity is what fuels the drives. In other words, the way a buyer thinks of himself or herself can actually push that person to acquire certain things, bond with certain people, search for certain insights and defend certain things. For instance, if being financially successful is part of your personal identity, you will seek to acquire things that prove to you and those around you that you are indeed financially successful. If you were to say, "In my life, family comes before career," you may not seek to acquire any of the possessions or experiences that indicate financial success. You instead would seek to acquire experiences that bring your family together.

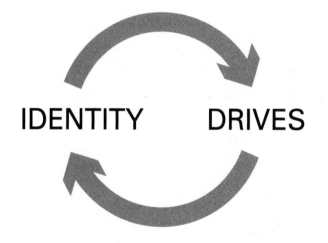

IDENTITY   DRIVES

Identity/drives cycle

Your identity feeds your drives, which in turn shape your identity. And on the process goes.

If being a powerful player is part of your personal identity, you will seek to bond with people in positions of influence. If being hopeless was to form part of your identity, you would avoid those very same people.

One of the most powerful ways to influence buyers is to have some idea of how they see themselves, how they want you to see them and through which criteria they judge themselves. These are key points, so let me repeat them:

- How the buyers see themselves.
- How the buyers want you to see them.
- How the buyers judge themselves.

I need to return to the fact here that if you want to influence the buyers, you need to get them to like you. You need them to perceive you as either being like them or being like they want other people to see them. And how they go about forming that perception is through certain criteria that they judge as being important. Very shortly, I will actually categorize the criteria that buyers use, but just before I do let me get a little clearer on how we construct this "identity" I keep talking about.

Most psychologists would agree that we develop our sense of identity from three perspectives. Firstly, we have a view of ourselves. Secondly, we have an opinion about how others see us. And thirdly, we have something that we aspire to be.

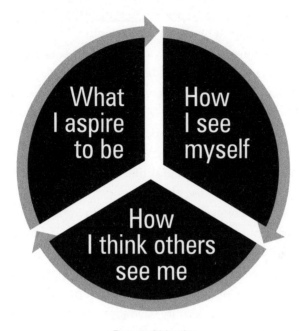

Personal identity

If you want to know what gives rise to motivation (think the four drives), it is the misalignment among these things.

If I feel that others don't think I am as successful as I think I am or want to be, I will seek to acquire possessions that make me look successful. I will attempt to bond with people who are obviously successful and will learn about the things successful people understand, such as the stock market.

If I feel that I am not as generous as I want to be, I might make a donation and buy one of the rubber bracelets that is both a public display and a personal reminder that I am generous (as well as being an advertisement for the

209

cause). If I think others see me as being more loving to my family than I am, I might try to do things that support that opinion. I might coach my son's football team. I might take the family on regular holidays. All in the name of upholding the positive identity I believe others have of me.

I think you get the point. The misalignment among the elements that make up our identity drives us to bond with people and brands, acquire possessions, services and experiences, and learn new things that will create greater congruence between those elements.

It is the incongruence that presents us with the biggest opportunity to get the buyer to exchange. If you know what the aspiration is, what the buyer's identity is and how he or she wants to be perceived, you can position both yourself and your offer as a potential supporter of those beliefs, or as an opportunity to improve their alignment.

I cannot tell you how excited I am just writing this. The power to be gained from understanding this notion of identity cannot be overemphasized. Influence is where the rubber meets the road on your journey to making it happen. And at the heart of your ability to influence is your ability to be liked or admired by the buyer. Just knowing how buyers see themselves offers an instant window into their "hot buttons." It is why being desperate can kill your ability to influence. No one likes or wants to be like a desperate person. And, as you are about to discover, they are not very hard to spot if you know what the possibilities are and you are looking and listening hard enough.

210

Banwari Mittal of Northern Kentucky University has written an outstanding essay on the six different lenses through which we judge ourselves, and here they are:

1. **Our bodies:** Our physical appearance, looks, the clothes we wear, our level of fitness and so on.
2. **Our values and character:** What we judge as being important to us and how we behave.
3. **Our competence and success:** What we have achieved, our professional and social standing and the wealth we have accumulated.
4. **Our social roles:** The roles we play in our life, including family, friends and broader associations. We could be a mother, a daughter, a coach, a leader, a creator, an artist and so on.
5. **Our subjective personality traits:** How we behave. Are we extroverted, passionate, shy, clumsy? And on the list could go.
6. **Our possessions:** What have we got? What car do we drive? What sort of house do we live in?

Now here comes the kicker: the buyer will judge you through the very same lens by which he or she judges himself or herself. When you come face to face with a buyer, he or she will be asking some very important questions, whether consciously or not:

- Is this seller worthy of my attention? In other words, is there some alignment between who I am and who I think they are?
- Does this seller represent something I want to be?
- How will others perceive me if I am engaged with this seller?
- How does the seller perceive me?

211

If the buyer values possessions, he or she will judge your worthiness by the same thing. If the buyer is a fitness freak, he or she will judge you on the physical state of your body. If the buyer cares deeply about family, he or she will pass judgment on you about how clearly you value your family above all else, if you have one. If the buyer values getting the job done at any expense, he or she will decide to partner with you if achievement and success are equally as powerful in your life.

This is why in Rapport 101 they tell you to engage in small talk: so you can find some common ground. You could gain the same insight by noticing other things about your potential buyers too: the time and length of their emails; when they make themselves available to meet; whether they want to relax over lunch or offer you 20 minutes; what event or forum they were attending when you met them; what they have on the walls around their office; what their demeanor with their PA is like; what sort of questions they ask you about your life and your work; whether or not they enquire about your family; whether they talk about their kids or their share portfolio.

The great irony in all of this is that everyone is going through the same process at exactly the same time. I like to joke about the fact that we walk down the street thinking everyone is judging us when the truth is they are not judging us, they are too concerned with the belief that we are judging them.

If you want to be easy to like, you need to:

- Make it clear that you perceive the buyer in the way you think he or she wants to be perceived—

212

that is, compliment him or her on the features he or she is clearly investing in showing the world.

- Show how bonding with you will at the very least support the identity the buyer has of himself or herself and at best help the buyer to become even more than what he or she is now. If he or she is into health, talk about some of the things you do to stay fit, or if not you then one of your closest friends.

- Emphasize your quality in the area that the buyer uses as a yardstick by which to judge himself or herself. If he or she likes fashion, talk about the brands that you love.

This is why I believe so deeply in the concept of playing the game. Remember, way back at the start I said that life is basically a series of exchanges, a big game, in a way. I revisited the idea under the heading of "Appearance" in being "Easy to Believe" as well. No one is above this game. No one! If you are doing business in a market where the way you look matters, you need to pay attention to this. You are not so cool and so powerful that you are beyond playing the game. Well, at least not yet. If your market measures everything by the bottom line, then don't come in waving your finger saying all your company needs to care about is making people happy. Trust me when I tell you it is easier to influence someone when he or she believes in and likes you. When you have rapport, amazing things can happen. When you don't, you are dead in the water. Influence is a subtle process. You don't just come in and force a new model on the

213

buyer's world. You dance and play and slowly engage the buyer in seeing a new possibility. If you go too hard too early and force your idea onto the buyer, and don't do so in a way that converts him or her to the belief that your view of the world is a better view, then you will incite the buyer's drive to defend and he or she will do one of two things:

1. Outright reject you and your idea.
2. Attempt to reform and re-educate you.

If you play the game, and you can present a new idea and have the buyer believe in it, you will appeal to the drive to comprehend, the drive to acquire and the drive to bond, which will lead the buyer to . . . BUY FROM YOU!

One last caveat, though. My rule is to play the game as hard as I can without violating my personal values or sense of ethics. You don't "sell your soul" for the deal. EVER!

I am talking about simple things, not just ethical things, such as you have a client who is a fitness fanatic and treats his body like a temple. When you eat with him, you take the salad over the burger and fries every time. That is unless, of course, you are overweight and look quite obviously as if you have never ordered a salad in your life.

No matter how hard you try, you can't fake it. Smart buyers will see right through you, plus it is disingenuous, which I am pretty sure will violate your own sense of identity. But you can be smart in the way you emphasize the different elements of who you are and what you stand for. And you should do this. This is not inauthentic, it is just plain smart.

214

If you stay true to your core and be clear about your values, this will almost certainly incite the buyer's desire to bond with you anyway. Why? Well, as I have already said, people desperately want to be congruent, and someone who is authentic will very much fit into the category of someone who is worth emulating. If a buyer wants to be like you, then I can assure you they will engage with you.

11

THE SALE

DO YOU WANT chocolate cake or fruit salad for dessert?

Now remember the number 21, and say it over and over again in your head.

Do you want chocolate cake or fruit salad for dessert?

Now remember this number: 8073652. Say it over and over again in your head.

Do you want chocolate cake or fruit salad for dessert?

At this point, I know you think I am off my rocker, but what I just did was basically reproduce an experiment done to test the impact that cognitive load has on people's decision-making. As it turns out, when you only have to remember the two digits—which is easy enough, right?— your rational brain holds sway over your emotional one, and 59 percent of the people tested chose the healthier option as a consequence. If, however, some of your cognitive function is hijacked by having you remember seven digits, you are less likely to choose the healthy option, as only 37 percent of those tested did in this instance. It appears that the more our rational mind is occupied with logistics, timing, how to pay and the like, the more emotional our decision will be.

At first glance, this seems like a very favorable thing for the seller indeed, considering that much of the competency of Influence consists of inciting emotion. However, I want you to remember two things:

1. The safest option (drive to defend) for any buyer in the short term is to do nothing.
2. The buyer's default position is no!

If we make our offer too complicated, even when our buyers have made the decision to engage, they will let fear (proven to be the most powerful human emotion) drive their behavior, or simply default to no.

At the simplest level, your ability to maintain your influence throughout the sale requires that your offer be:

■ Easy to choose.
■ Easy to buy.
■ Easy to integrate.

I persist with the concept of being "easy" not as some attempt to be "cute," but rather to again reinforce just how important mental energy (and the buyer's fear of squandering it) has become in the process of getting someone to engage with you. If you want to make it hap-

217

pen, you need to make everything easy for the buyer. Mental energy is just as valuable a currency as time and money these days, and in the same way that you strive to be efficient and speedy in your delivery, while maintaining a price point that is affordable (but still profitable), you should also attempt to make both the offer and the transaction as easy as possible for the buyer in every way.

EASY TO CHOOSE

There are few behavioral economists as quirky or as interesting as Dan Ariely. In his numerous publications, and his blockbuster *Predictably Irrational*, he helps us to understand why we don't behave logically, and to choose what might be best for us. Outlined here is what has become one of his more famous experiments.

Do you like jam? I love jam, although I had not realized I had been so unadventurous when it came to the flavors of jam I would try. Ariely once conducted an experiment in a supermarket where on different days he displayed jams for people to try and then hopefully buy.

On the first day, he put out six varieties on the stand. This attracted some attention, but nothing like the day he had 24 out. All the color and variety of the 24 different jams generated lots of attention. Only the strange thing was, despite the excitement, the extra variety not only did not increase sales, it actually caused them to plummet.

When there were just six jams on display, some 30 percent of people bought. When there were 24, it was a mere three percent. In other words, by lessening the options,

218

and making it easier to choose, sales conversion was up tenfold.

Mind-blowing, right? Well, ask yourself, how easy is it to choose the best way to engage with you? Do you offer all sorts of different products and services, and all sorts of different options? I bet if you are getting started you probably do. Why? Because we want to have something for everyone, remember? We cast the net wide hoping to hit the hot button of each and every buyer. The problem is, there comes a point where too much choice actually paralyzes the buyers. After all your work to get their attention and incite their intention, after all the work you did to make them believe in you and buy from you, they did not engage. Not because they didn't want to, but because they were too confused to.

Our friends at Salesforce.com, of course, nailed this too. They actually made it so easy to choose that you would be nuts not to try their online CRM product. Why? It was free. They had both a personal use version to get individuals hooked on Salesforce.com and a trial offer for larger business offerings.

They also tiered their engagement options. Depending on size, features you require, need to have access when offline, mobile device access requirements and the like you could choose the most cost-effective option that met your needs. You could do the very same thing.

Here is what I recommend. Whatever your idea, whatever you offer, whatever you are trying to engage the buyer in, offer it in three very simple packages: silver, gold, and platinum. Silver is the basic, gold is silver plus more, and platinum is gold plus more again. And stack

219

the value as you go from silver to gold and gold to platinum. If the gold package is 20 percent more expensive, make sure it has 40 percent more value.

What you will find is that most people will go for at least gold. Firstly, it represents better value, and secondly they probably have an identity that says they are not a tight-ass. This has been my experience, anyway.

The other reason you want to add more value is that in the early days of building engagement around your idea, be it customers for your business, or donors for your cause, the cost of acquisition is very high for you indeed. We usually underestimate just how much time, money and energy it takes to get someone over the line. Getting an extra 20 percent from him or her could be far more profitable for you than saving the extra time that the 40 percent more value represents. Plus, if you knock the socks off the buyer, he or she will keep buying from you and tell his or her friends to as well.

I'll give you an example. Let's say you are trying to start a business selling fishing expeditions. The silver package could include the boat hire, the guide, and the tackle and basic bait. This may be $400. But for $500 your buyers could get the gold package, which incorporates all of the silver package, plus better bait, breakfast, lunch, and dinner, and a shuttle service to and from the hotel. However, the platinum package, which is $750, incorporates all of the gold package and a specialist fishing instructor who will coach each customer individually to make them more effective fishers. You will go to a locals-only fishing spot and have a photo taken with your biggest catch of the day.

I know of a specialist estate agent who does exactly this with his property-management services. While his competitors are getting on average six percent of total rent as management fees, he is averaging above nine percent.

I think you get the point. These three packages would be better than having ten or so different options all listed with different prices and offering a multi-selection discount that scaled depending on how many options they chose. Why do you think the Value Meal deals work so well at McDonald's?

In truth, your offering may be a little more complex. And it is quite possible that it involves no transaction at all. Maybe you are the coordinator of aid missions to Africa, and it is not as simple as just buying a package. No matter what your idea, and no matter who you are trying to influence, you need to make it easy for them. You are still a sales consultant of sorts.

I know, personally, that when I shop, I value highly the recommendation of the person making the sale. Nothing is more frustrating than meeting a sales consultant who either does not really know enough about his or her product to make a recommendation or won't out of fear he or she will give you the wrong advice. It has been said countless times, people don't like to be sold to, but they love to buy. People do love to buy, but they need your help in deciding.

I believe you have an obligation to suggest to your client what he or she needs to engage with. Seriously, it is negligent to let the client choose a course of action that won't solve his or her problem. You must offer advice, especially if your offer attempts to solve highly complex

221

issues, in areas seldom fully understood by the buyer. They are buying into your expertise, not just buying from your offer.

This is why the notion that the customer is always right is so ridiculous. I think we have all moved on from that, and now customers want partners and advisers, not sellers. They want to co-create the solution, not be left to their own devices.

No one knows more about what you are offering than you—and least of all the buyer. If the buyer wants to engage you for a month, and you know he or she needs three, push for three. If the buyer says he or she will attend your church for one celebration of mass, suggest he or she at least gives it a month. Whatever it is, the buyer will value your knowledge and your contribution to the decision-making process. The easier you make it, the more likely he or she will be to engage.

EASY TO BUY

At the simplest level, being easy to buy is making sure that engaging you is so seamless it happens in a heartbeat. If you are seeking money, make sure that you accept payment by any possible means. If you are looking for a time commitment, either have the schedule all laid out or allow the buyer to choose when and where on the spot.

This may sound like such an obvious thing, but trust me it is not. I cannot pay my health insurance on the internet. I cannot pay it in advance by more than a month with a credit card. And my insurer has no direct-debit option. Checks are preferred. Freakin' checks. It is completely non-user-friendly. I remember not being able to get cable TV because I had no credit history in the U.S., and my offer to pay in advance for 12 months was not acceptable. I mean, there I was trying to give the company money and its payment systems wouldn't allow it.

These examples are from the realm of big bureaucracies, but your smaller outfit could be the same. Do you take all forms of credit card? Do you have a direct-debit plan? And these are just the basics. Depending on the buyer, you might find yourself needing to do a lot of things to make your idea easy to buy. Let me share another personal example with you.

When I first started selling my school seminars, I soon realized that I needed to focus mostly on government schools. I found, ironically, that the buyers at private schools were much harder to get to, and because it was generally perceived that they had more money, they were also more constantly bombarded.

With the government schools, I worked out very quickly that the biggest objection was not to the contention that student motivation and lack of study skills was a problem, or that I could genuinely solve that problem, but that there was no way of paying for it. In other words, I had done a good job of positioning the need, but there was no point if people couldn't actually buy.

After chatting to a few schools, I learned about some government funding that all government schools had access to called School to Work funding. This funding was significant but required that schools apply for it, and that the activity being paid for would in some way assist stu-

223

dents in making the transition from school to work. I got a copy of one of the grant submissions and repackaged my brochure with an increased emphasis on the career-selection components of my main talk, and even used the words "school to work" throughout my session descriptions.

This was the government equivalent of a trend. And in a matter of days my conversion rates shot up. Now I not only could identify a problem, and one that was most relevant at that time of the year, I also had a solution and even an answer to the buyers' biggest problem: How will I pay for it? In summary, I positioned my offering and expertise around the criteria for funding, in this case the transition from school to work.

You need to make sure it is easy to buy from you. Is it? How could you make it even easier?

EASY TO INTEGRATE

Let me just state right now that I love Macs and PCs equally. Seriously, I have both and I like them for different reasons. So what I am about to say is not Microsoft bashing, and nor am I the first to say it.

As soon as Office 2007 became available, I bought it. A challenging time lay ahead, let me assure you. By default, I was creating documents in Word 2007 format and sending them to my clients. Inevitably, the clients were coming back to me with problems such as, "The file is corrupt. There are no words when I open it."

After some frustration and some searching of online computer forums, I found out that people with Word

224

2003 cannot open Word 2007 documents unless they go to the Microsoft website and download a "patch." Remember, these are two products from the same company. Two years after I first started using 2007, I was still having this problem. And don't get me started on the problems I had with drivers when I first upgraded to Vista (which, by the way, I thought was as good an operating system as XP, despite what people said).

You see, both products were awesome. They had features I valued. I was compelled to pay top dollar for the chance to use them. What went wrong is that they were a nightmare to integrate. So here I am, an avid fan who now can't help but complain about how frustrating his user experience has been.

This is no different from people telling you when they will deliver your product but giving you an eight-hour window with no guarantee that they will stick to it and a refusal to call upon arrival. Whatever you are offering, make sure it integrates well into the life of the buyer. Do not in your frantic push to get some buyers engaged forget how you are going to make the integration of your offering seamless to them.

Be easy to choose, easy to buy and easy to integrate, and you will ensure that the sale is not a barrier to engagement. Only today, as I make the final edits on this, the U.S. edition of the book, I was on a coaching call with a benefits broker in Palo Alto, CA. They have a total of 17 prospects in their pipeline who openly say they think that their company has a better process, and offers far superior service. Yet still they won't engage. Why? The collateral damage and stress that changing benefits brokers will

225

cause. The suggestions we brainstormed on the call was to create a specialist "transition team" which for a moderate fee will project manage the data transfer, conduct seminars and training on the new systems and create customized reports that talk to existing company reporting processes and structures.

Many of the strategies outlined here under the competency of Influence are about removing the barrier to engagement. Whether it be physical or character issues that rub the buyer the wrong way, whether it be fear and risk that you need to mitigate, or whether it be logistical aspects relating to how the client can buy and integrate your offer, you need to make this process as easy as possible.

This requires that you take on a great deal of complexity yourself. Just understanding the identity of the buyer, and the way personal identity interacts with the four human drives, requires a great deal of insight. Designing your packages and the way they integrate to be easy throughout the sales process takes work too. Do the work! The buyer will thank you for it, and you will have won your first victory. Your idea has just become a reality. The buyer has bought! You just made it happen!

MAKING INFLUENCE HAPPEN

▶ Get clear and focus on the story you believe the buyers will tell themselves about why they want/need to buy from you.

▶ Develop and communicate clearly "stuff" such as features and benefits that would make it easy for a buyer to justify that "story"-driven decision to engage with you instead of somebody else.

▶ Know and subliminally communicate how your offer meets the specific buyer's drive to acquire, bond, comprehend and defend.

▶ Work tirelessly to find ways to measure the value you bring.

▶ Be passionate and persistent when offering your product—if you don't believe in yourself and your offer, the buyer won't either.

▶ Seek referrals where possible and capture all quality testimonials about the value you bring.

▶ Increase the value of what you do by offering guarantees, charging a premium price if appropriate, and stop trying to convince everyone you meet to buy from you.

▶ Play the game by paying obsessive attention to the way you "show up." Your appearance and other first impressions may be the difference between closing the deal and not.

▶ Quickly identify the filters that your buyer uses to define his or her own identity and focus in on how you and your offer represent something aspirational in your buyer's preferred area.

▶ Facilitate the process when the time comes to engage by being easy to choose, easy to buy and easy to integrate for the buyer.

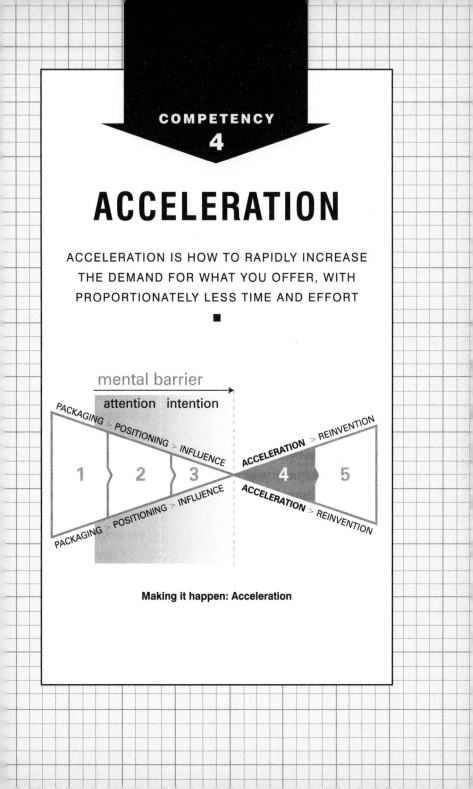

COMPETENCY
4

ACCELERATION

ACCELERATION IS HOW TO RAPIDLY INCREASE
THE DEMAND FOR WHAT YOU OFFER, WITH
PROPORTIONATELY LESS TIME AND EFFORT

■

mental barrier

attention   intention

PACKAGING > POSITIONING > INFLUENCE

1   2   3   4   5

ACCELERATION > REINVENTION

PACKAGING > POSITIONING > INFLUENCE

ACCELERATION > REINVENTION

Making it happen: Acceleration

12

CREATING LEVERAGE

RIGHT ABOUT NOW, you should really take a moment to stop and congratulate yourself. You have effectively made the sale. You are on the right-hand side of a buyer's mental barrier. Okay—now stop celebrating! What you need to do next is to get on the right-hand side of lots of buyers' mental barriers, and you want to make sure it takes much less time and effort than this first sale has taken. You want it to happen easily and you want it to happen fast. Well, the good news is that it can, but you will have to stop congratulating yourself and get back to work. The enemy of great is good, as they say. Well, the enemy of really making it happen is self-satisfaction.

I know you have a permanent dissatisfaction that simmers below the surface, that always makes you want to do and learn more. That is part of who you are and what attracted you to this book. Well, that is a blessing on the road to making it happen. It may make you a right pain in the neck to live with, but trust me when I tell you it will make you successful. It is this dissatisfaction that will ensure you don't rest on your laurels and play small. And the cool thing is that, now you are on the right-hand side, where you have credibility and are seen as authentic, you are in the circle of trust.

If you can accelerate the uptake of your offer, or have it taken up by more lucrative buyers, and better still get a greater value of exchange for it, then you will massively increase your success. You should not necessarily interpret success here as making more money. You will certainly do that, but more important I think is that you will have a greater impact. There are levels that you progress through as you master the Acceleration competency, and I call these the five levels of impact. Every level you climb brings you a greater impact (better results), with the same or even less investment of time, money and energy.

I must say here that I don't think you ever really master Acceleration. You get better at it and you can move up the levels of impact, but there is always more. Always. I have only really started to truly understand the power of this competency in the last couple of years, and I have to tell you it has been a revelation. If I had known ten years ago what I know now, my impact would have been exponentially greater than it has been to date.

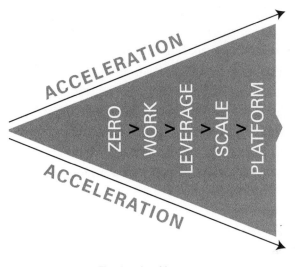

Five levels of impact

- **Zero level:** When you are first trying to make it happen, you have virtually zero impact. No one is listening and no one is buying.
- **Work level:** Once you master packaging, positioning and influence, you are at least making a difference. But in reality it is still work. You are exchanging effort for a proportional return.
- **Leverage level:** When you have leverage, you are able to command a disproportionate return for your effort. Instead of exchanging time and effort for money, you are exchanging "value" for money.
- **Scale level:** I love scale. This is where you are able to get a return on other people's effort. And although it is proportional return, you still get disproportionately rewarded because you are no longer limited by your own time. At scale, you can get

233

multiple returns, which together give you a highly disproportionate return on your time and effort.

- **Platform level:** This is where the big kids play. When you have platform, you no longer have to exchange anything that resembles time, energy or effort. Now your brand itself, or the intellectual property you have created, is so powerful that you simply license it to other people who get leverage and scale with it, giving you a piece of a much, much bigger pie.

Acceleration is about moving up all the levels to platform level, and for now we are focused on leverage. I have three specific strategies I want to share with you on your road to getting leverage. These are:

1. Seizing your moments of mass exposure.
2. Targeting more lucrative buyers.
3. Measuring and billing for output, not input.

SEIZING YOUR MOMENTS OF MASS EXPOSURE

During his time at Queens College, New York, Jerry Seinfeld participated in some college productions. This piqued his interest in stand-up comedy and, like so many others who had gone before him, he tried out at an open-mic night called Catch a Rising Star. The year was 1976. He was not an overnight hit, but he enjoyed it enough to keep on going. After a few years schlepping it on the stand-up scene, he had a bit of a breakthrough when he

234

appeared a couple of times on the sitcom *Benson*. No doubt, this small level of visibility acted as an accelerant on his success.

I can't imagine these small parts really took as much work as developing a stand-up routine, yet the exposure that TV could give him and the credibility it lent would have immediately bumped up his popularity as a comedian. He could do one piece of work and expose it to hundreds of thousands more people. This was Jerry's first big break, as they say.

On his merry way he continued, working extremely hard, as we have previously discussed, until someone threw gasoline on the flame that was Jerry's stand-up career. And that gasoline came in the form of a highly successful appearance on *The Tonight Show Starring Johnny Carson* in 1981. This would be a day that would change his world.

You will find yourself at key moments in time that could be the difference between reasonable success and truly making it big. I call them moments of mass exposure. Seinfeld's was *The Tonight Show.*

Seinfeld knew the importance of his upcoming TV appearance as a comic on *The Tonight Show* so he went to work. And this is the key lesson. He was already a very good comedian. If he was not, he would not have been asked on. Yet he went to work again anyway. What I have seen too many people do is rely on the fact that they are good, and therefore never make the big splash they could make when given a key moment of opportunity. It is as though our small level of success to date allows us to get cocky and we stop raising the bar. Compared with our

235

friends and family, we have made it. We started with our idea and now we have some sales. We feel like we have already made it happen. This mindset is toxic, because there is always more you could be doing, and there is always room to improve. This sort of behavior could be called self-sabotage.

Do not let your early wins make you complacent or cocky. Don't let your growing confidence rob you of the very humility that made you "do the work." And do not let your growing success make you too busy to grab these key moments when they appear. Jerry Seinfeld didn't, and that is why he is, well, Jerry Seinfeld.

Seinfeld started delivering literally dozens of performances for well below his appearance fee in comedy clubs around New York so he could fine-tune his set. He was not too proud, and he knew this small sacrifice of time and money would pay off if he aced the Carson appearance. And that he did. So successful was it that he was invited back and onto other shows as well. Before too long, he had a regular gig on Dave Letterman's show. His stand-up career flourished with this newfound exposure, and he was shortly thereafter named the number-12 best stand-up comedian ever.

As a result of all this, he got leverage. With one initial television appearance, he was able to build his reputation as a comedian much faster than if he had to trek from live gig to live gig. Instead of building his audiences hundreds of people at a time, he was now building literally millions of people at a time. His popularity soared. Now, he had more offers to perform coming through his door than he knew what to do with, and they came with disproportionately less effort than all the ones that had come before.

Jerry had seized his moment of mass exposure, and you can too. The question is, where do you find it? That really depends on what you are trying to build. The lesson here is to go looking for your moments of opportunity, and don't wait for them to come to you. And when you get them, put everything into making them a success. Consider the following questions to get you started:

- Where do your buyers meet? And how can you get in front of them or become part of their environment?
- What do your buyers read? How can you contribute to this publication?
- What clients can you get who would not only create massive internal opportunities for you but also open up a whole new world of opportunity through their network and through the credibility that having them confers?
- Who are the influencers among your buyers? How can you develop a relationship with them?

TARGETING MORE LUCRATIVE BUYERS

Now that Jerry Seinfeld was a household name all of a sudden, instead of performing to small crowds in comedy clubs around New York, he was booking out theatres across the country. I have no idea what his appearance fee was, but it could have easily been ten times higher than it was before

237

his *Tonight Show* success. His ability to seize his moment had allowed him to target a much more lucrative buyer.

It is here that Salesforce.com started to really make their money. The marginal increase in cost for having 10,000 users instead of 9,000 is minimal for a business like Salesforce.com. In the early days, to establish their credibility and iron out the cracks, they aggressively pursued small and medium businesses. However, the plan was always to take on the big guys for enterprise level adoption. The sales team at Johnson & Johnson is literally thousands of times larger than a small to medium business, and yet the extra customization and additional pressure on the server and online software is minimal.

In order to go after these more lucrative enterprise buyers, they needed different kinds of sales processes themselves and different kinds of people. So they started to poach key sales people from a wide variety of big IT players which included SAP, PeopleSoft, and the like. These people knew how to sell to and get access to the large enterprise buyers. In many cases, they had sold traditional CRM solutions to these very same clients. The business got a kick overnight, and margins improved.

Their offer also had to improve to win these more lucrative clients, and as they were making this push in 2003/2004, they made key upgrades that include Outlook integration, workflow, calendaring and team-selling. All key requirements of the enterprise buyer. They also achieved scale through other people efforts, but before showing how they did this let me share with you the best idea I have for getting a greater return on your time and effort: to stop billing clients for time and effort!

238

MEASURING AND BILLING FOR OUTPUT, NOT INPUT

What is the problem with charging per hour? There are only 24 of them in a day! Seriously, if you charge by inputs such as hours worked, then there will be a cap placed on your reward. I will use money as my prime example for this strategy.

There is only so much you can charge when you are suggesting to a buyer that your value is in the hours you work. Sure, you can charge a lot for an hour these days, as lawyers, accountants and many consultants do—perhaps even as much as $1000 per hour, as some of the very best attorneys in the U.S. do. But your success is capped.

Let's say you are one of those attorneys and you are getting $1000 per billable hour. Let's assume you bill around 50 hours per week for 50 weeks a year. Your return is capped at $2.5 million. Now, that may seem like a nice return to you now, but trust me when I tell you that once you master this competency, it will seem like way too much work for that return. I am not trying to be glib here. Rather, I am trying to open your mind to what Acceleration can offer.

Let's imagine that throughout the course of that year you were to save corporations $200 million worth of damages claims, and a further $50 million worth of future damages claims through your excellent lawyering skills. At $2.5 million, you got a one percent return on the value you brought to those clients. Do you think you brought massive value? Yes! So why not bill for it? Why not take the risk of no return on your time and effort and do a deal

239

with the client that is equal to five percent of the immediate savings and two percent of the agreed future savings you can bring them?

Your fee would be $10 million for the current savings and $1 million for the future savings. You just took a $2.5 million return and made it $11 million for no extra effort. Sure, if you added no value you would get nothing, but if you truly believe in the exchange of value then you deserved nothing.

I have massively simplified this example and I have made some even bigger assumptions. One is that you can actually add this much value, and two that the client can't find someone else who is just as capable and will do it for less (even by the hour). But the example is still valid.

Lawyers the world over when working with compensation victims often work for free and can take up to fifty percent of the damages they manage to sue for.

If you get a $2 million pay out, they can (and do) charge $1 million for getting you that return. It may have taken only 100 hours to get it for you, but instead of getting $1000 for each of those hours they actually get $10,000 per hour. As an important aside, this practice is part of what is destroying the legal system and leading to a litigious culture, so I am not a huge fan of how it has been used in regard to personal responsibility and litigation, but as a principle for making it happen it is pure gold.

Why do you think investment banks and stock traders make so much money? Because they don't bill per hour; they bill a percentage of the value they bring. If they do a multi-billion-dollar acquisition, their fee will be a percentage of the deal. If they make a trade for you on $100,000, they take a percentage of that trade, even if executing that trade only took a few seconds. Or what about when the GM building in midtown Manhattan sold for $2.8 billion in 2008? The commercial real-estate company that managed that transaction would have got a percentage fee of the value. In other words, it would have billed for output and not for input, and you should look to see how you might be able to do the same.

There is something else that these examples have in common: they all involve value that can easily be measured in dollar terms. You may want to return to the section on metrics: the easier it is to measure the value you bring, the easier it is for the client to justify engaging with you. Well, let me add to that here by saying that the easier it will be for you to charge fairly for it as well. And, to finish with the example with which we started—Jerry Seinfeld—as his success grew he was not just able to charge more but, like many artists who had preceded him, also to start charging a percentage of door-ticket sales as well. In other words, he was getting compensated at an amount commensurate with the value he could bring, measured in ticket sales—again, doing the same amount of work and getting a much higher return.

How could you do the same?

GETTING SCALE

DO YOU REMEMBER when you were younger trying
to figure out among your friends whether Superman would
beat Batman in a fight? Maybe this is a boy thing, but I
always wondered whether The Hulk could get the better
of The Phantom. As I grew up, my friends and I shifted
our focus from superheroes to forms of martial arts. Is
karate better than tae kwon do? Or would a judo black-
belt beat a champion boxer? Well, as it turns out we were
not the only ones thinking along these lines, only we did
not manage to turn it into a massive global phenomenon.

In the early 1990s, while doing some research into
martial arts for a client, ad man Art Davie met Rorion
Gracie, a master of Brazilian ju-jitsu. Not only was Gracie
interested in what was the best martial art but also he was
a frequent participant in an age-old Brazilian tradition of

242

actually fighting in interdisciplinary matches. In fact, Gracie had even made a video series of himself and other members of his martial-arts-mad family defeating masters of various martial arts.

Davie had an idea. He proposed to Rorion and a screenwriter buddy—John Milius—that they actually stage an event that would answer the question of which was the best martial art. Only Davie did not think small. Right from the outset, he was thinking scale. He wanted the event to be on TV. He wanted to call it *War of the Worlds*.

It took some serious work. Davie had to package, position and influence 28 investors to get the financial backing for the show. It was obviously not everyone's idea of wholesome family entertainment. He called the company WOW Productions.

After coming up against a lot of closed doors, the WOW team managed to convince pay-per-view specialists Semaphore Entertainment Group to air the event, which came to be known as the Ultimate Fighting Championships 1, or UFC 1 for short. Denver, Colorado, was the lucky host city.

So was it a success? Did they manage to get enough people to pay to watch this event? Well, you know the answer is going to be yes, but herein lies a strategy for getting to the level of scale: the power of viral marketing—or, put simply, word of mouth.

GOING VIRAL

UFC was so different, so outrageous, and so able to answer a testosterone-induced question asked by boys the world over that word could not help but spread. This was in the days before the explosion of the internet, so it is not as if they could have just uploaded a YouTube clip and watched it spread like wildfire. This was good, old-fashioned word of mouth. Almost 86,000 people paid to see this event on cable television—an instant success, which brought with it outrage from people all over America. Among the offended was Senator John McCain, who made it his mission to shut down this form of "human cockfighting."

Today, with Web 2.0 and the social-networking tools available, it is even easier to go viral. If you want to refresh your memory on how powerful this can be, go back and check out the piece on "Will it Blend" in Chapter 7, Moving the Market.

Whenever you have a good experience in a restaurant, how many people do you tell? Two to three roughly. If you have a bad experience, how many do you tell? Perhaps ten to 13. This is what has long been known as word of mouth. Only now it is not word of mouth, but word of mouse.

Not all viral campaigns have to go on the internet, as UFC indicates. Have you ever seen someone on a plane wearing those Bose sound-minimizing headphones? Well, in anticipation of the curiosity that the company hoped the headphones would provoke in onlookers, Bose included a small pile of cards in the case that you could hand to fellow passengers. Considering I have seen these headphones everywhere, I think it is fair to say they went viral.

What I like about the Bose example is that it is analog, yet still the brand made sure it was easy to spread the word. How can you make it easy for your buyers to spread the word? Or how can you start the virus yourself?

For now, let's return to the UFC. The outrage that followed the 1993 event in Colorado was just what the promoters wanted. The tagline of the UFC—"There are no rules"—was anti-establishment in such a big way that even if this sort of violence was not your thing, it was hard not to talk about it. And talk about it they did. Within just a few years, 36 American states had banned any such event from being held within its borders, and the much bigger cable TV channels resisted the temptation to get behind this pay-per-view phenomenon. As it turns out, even the UFC knew how to play the game, so it did.

It introduced more rules, was sanctioned by various athletic commissions and managed to gain much wider mainstream television support. Some of the rules actually already existed, but it needed to tidy up its image a little (without becoming too clean) if it was to get the backing of the bigger media properties it sought. Remember that, from day one, this was meant to be massive, and TV was its vehicle. This is another strategy for attaining scale.

MAINSTREAM MEDIA

So much has been said and written about the death of TV. I think its demise is being massively overplayed and the mainstream media is still the number-one place to go to get lots of eyeballs. Sure, the internet has almost a zero price of entry, but as a result there is so much content out there that it is much more likely your message will get lost in the mess. Every minute, 60 new hours of video are uploaded to YouTube.

245

Whether it be TV, radio, film, or print, getting exposure in mainstream media can really accelerate your movement up the levels of impact, and you will find yourself at the level of scale much faster than if you had not got this coverage. You may even consider getting a professional PR person to manage this. My experience is that it is well worth the investment.

For the UFC, the big wins included ESPN coverage, features on Fox Sports Net, a cameo for famed fighter Chuck Liddell on Entourage and being featured in reality show *American Casino*. Now, be warned: this go-big-fast strategy was neither fast nor cheap. A decade on, more money was still being put into the UFC than was being taken out (it had been sold to another entity at this point). The new UFC team decided to take things into their own hands and made a self-funded reality TV show called *The Ultimate Fighter*. The first pay-per-view event to follow this had more than 280,000 subscribers, and that is to say nothing of the success of the show itself. In 2006, the year that followed the show's release, the UFC broke all the records for pay-per-view numbers, with events now getting more than a million subscribers, beating boxing and even the WWF. Revenues in 2006 were over $220 million. UFC had popped, and it was now spinning off other multimillion-dollar franchises.

In the two years that followed, scale ensued in a big way, with sponsorships from both Budweiser and Harley-Davidson. This is what you call platform—a brand so powerful that it draws opportunity to it, without any extra work. More on that in a moment, and for now here are two more strategies for attaining scale.

PARTNER

Not everyone will match the success of the UFC, and there is every chance your idea does not really have that sort of mainstream-media potential either. If this is the case, finding the right partner can be a very fast and potent way of moving up to the impact level of scale.

What if you are selling breakfast cereal? How would you like to turn your passion for organic food into a business that you can then sell for more than $120 million in just five years? That is what Connecticut-born food-lovers Brendan Synnott and Kelly Flatley did.

Kelly loved to cook, and her friends loved the way she cooked. She started making her own granola in college and further honed her craft in the first couple of years of her post-college life. It turned out that she liked making granola more than she liked work. So, at 23, she decided to try to make it a business. By night, she would mix and bake her granola and by day she would go to fresh-food markets, small, independent health-food stores, and anywhere else she could think of and sell her granola one bag at a time. She had neither leverage nor scale at this point.

Just one month into this new lifestyle, Kelly bumped into her high-school buddy Brendan Synnott, who was working in TV in New York at the time. He was so juiced by Kelly's little, as yet not financially successful, venture that he took a leave of absence from which he would never return to help her bake and sell this world-class granola. Between them, they were able to bake more than 45 kilograms of it every night. This only really has significance when you realize it was still being made in Kelly's apartment kitchen.

No one apart from small health-food-shop-owners had any clue who they were or what they did, so they went door to door at community fairs and local markets offering samples of their homemade granola. The year was 2002. They were making no money at this point, yet Brendan decided not to return to his job working for *Saturday Night Live*, and both put their life savings into the new venture—a whopping $7,000. Neither were really making an income, so both were forced to move back home with their parents in Darien, Connecticut. Their office was the spare bedroom of Kelly's parents' house, and for the next 18 months they took no salary from the business at all. Talk about holding your nerve.

Kelly and Brendan knew this was unsustainable. They needed scale, and the only way to get it was by partnering with a large grocery chain. They targeted Stew Leonard's, a local supermarket chain in Connecticut, but the head buyer wouldn't even return their calls. Out of desperation, they decided to stalk him by bringing him breakfast one morning at the store. They were devastated to learn that he was away on holiday, but as luck would have it the store owner saw them and was so intrigued by their approach he agreed to take a meeting and try their cereal. He ordered 50 cases on the spot—their largest order to date.

248

Now they had scale. Next came The Food Emporium in New York City, and with it 40 new stores serving health-conscious, hungry New Yorkers. The story continued until the pair found themselves $100,000 in debt with maxed-out credit cards, so they brought on an investor. The extra capital allowed them to move to a bigger facility and put on more staff, and before long they were servicing 25 states. This was just two years after they'd started.

Sam's Club, Target, Publix, Safeway, and Whole Foods were added to their list of partners, and now they were coast to coast in the U.S. and found out their Bear Naked brand boasted the number-one and number-two bestselling granola products in America. It was four years since they had started. The following year, they sold Bear Naked to a subsidiary of Kellogg's for $122 million—not bad for a couple of 23-year-olds who hated their jobs.

Kelly and Brendan got scale because they found the right distribution and financial partners at the right time. Here are some questions for you to ponder, if scale is something you are pursuing:

Who could you partner with to distribute your offer? Who represents the right brand and scale for you at this point in time?

Is there someone you could work with who brings either a network, capital, or experience you could use?

RECRUIT, TRAIN, AND GROW

This almost sounds too simple a point to even mention, but it does need saying. I cannot tell you how many businesses I know whose growth was strangled because the owner was too tight to bring someone on. You cannot make it all about you if you want scale. And I am not only talking about bringing on employees. Let's look at an example of an organization that has achieved scale without actually hiring or paying people.

I am constantly surprised at what people will do for free. The drive to bond is so powerful that if people believe in you and your idea, they will give their time, money and energy just to feel a part of it. This is the premise on which the Landmark Forum has been built.

The company Landmark Education, headquartered in San Francisco, is now in more than 115 countries and delivers public and company-based personal-development programs. There is no question the programs are brilliant, but it starts to feel a bit stifling the more you get into it.

Landmark doesn't talk about "recruitment"; it calls it enrollment. The flagship event is called the Landmark Forum, and it is built on the work of Werner Erhard, who in the 1970s ran something called The Forum (which he had previously called Erhard Seminars Training, or EST). Basically, you go through a series of exercises that equate to group therapy. And I mean powerful group therapy.

As an attendee, I was taken by the experience, and it is only on reflection that I realized what they were doing closely resembled the training methodology used in the military to build cohesion. All the world's armed forces know that even hormone-crazed 18-year-olds won't charge up a hill against enemy fire for God and country. But they will do it to not let down the group to which they've become loyal and in which they find their strongest sense of identity (drive to bond). The process is to: a) establish control, b) break down or hijack pre-existing

250

bonds and sense of self; and c) instill a new sense of self in terms of new bonds.

Once the Landmark Forum session starts, you feel like you can't leave. I remember being unsure whether it was appropriate to use the bathroom. I am being a little dramatic, but there is a powerful set of unwritten expectations in Landmark events and an even more powerful group psychology, all of which is orchestrated by the extremely skilled facilitators who lead the Forum seminars. Now, thankfully they do not drive you out to some strange place and have you drink the Kool-Aid, but they do direct this newfound influence over you in pursuit of the scale that the organization seeks.

Having experienced Forum first hand, I would have to say I felt bullied into inviting at least two of my friends to the final night of the seminar, which occurs two or three nights later. This is made worse when they tell you that if you do not come with others you are deemed to not have graduated (tapping in to the drive to acquire, wouldn't you say?). Anyway, if you have ever tried to convince someone to attend a seminar with you, you will know they are often suspicious of your motivation.

Yet, for no compensation, people will adhere to the whole program. You pay to attend the Forum and then you are expected to do the marketing for the next one, or you won't graduate. And people do! With more than 200,000 people paying to attend the courses every year, you cannot deny its success. With current revenues likely to be over $100 million a year, it is at least nice to know the company is owned by the employees themselves, with no single person having a stake of more than three percent.

But it does not stop there. Once members have graduated, the most committed among them start volunteering, only they don't get to do cool stuff such as facilitate parts of the seminar. No, that takes more than seven years of service. Instead, they have to man the phones and make outbound sales calls to "enroll" people in the other seminars on offer at Landmark.

These are people who would most probably see it as beneath their dignity to work in a call center, however much they were paid, doing it now for free! Such is the power of the competency of Influence we discussed in the last part.

Who could you "enroll" into your cause? Open-source software has harnessed this very same desire to contribute and bind in a most powerful way.

At the very least, could you perhaps pay staff just to free up your time to do more leveraged activity, therefore increasing your speed to scale? Better still, could you bring people on who could deliver your offer, generate income and ultimately be a profit-producing asset for your business? The answer is obviously yes. Don't kill your cause by trying to extract a few thousand extra dollars out of your organization. It may end up costing you millions in less than a few years.

14

BUILDING PLATFORM

IF YOU HAVE ever traveled throughout Asia, Africa, Eastern Europe or South America, you would have been struck by the poverty you saw. You know it exists, but until you see it firsthand it is hard to know just how bad it is. And it is even harder once you have seen it not to want to do something about it.

At least, this is what happened to Blake Mycoskie. On a trip to Argentina, two things stuck out for this former contestant on *The Amazing Race*. One was the prevalence of a very basic but comfortable-looking shoe called the alpargata. The second was despite how basic these shoes were, there were scores of kids too poor to even afford a pair. Mycoskie had his idea. On his return to the U.S., he would give the alpargata a makeover, making it more attractive to U.S. customers, and for every pair he sold he would donate a pair to the poverty-stricken children of Argentina. Neat idea, don't you think? He called it Tom's Shoes.

Note how powerful the story is in this example. Remember, it's the private element that makes someone buy. Sure, the shoes were cool—or, as some customers would argue, "they were cool because the shoe itself was not"—but it was the story that surrounded the shoes that won the day. Even if you bought a pair and never wore them, it would still have been a good purchase because at the very least you would have contributed to the well-being of children in Argentina.

Blake was able to go from good idea to great results in just six months, selling 20,000 pairs of shoes. And in just four years, this little idea of his became a global enterprise, selling shoes on the one for one model. More than 600,000 shoes had been donated to young children between 2006 and 2010. Brilliant!

Now, think about this for a minute. In the space of four years, Blake's idea to help kids in Argentina own their first pair of shoes, so they could go to school, went from aspiration to reality. And not just for a few, but pushing 1 million. How did he make such an impact so quickly?

Well, let's start by admitting it is a bloody good idea. Giving people not only the chance to acquire some shoes but also a sense of well-being in knowing that they have helped a child in need satisfies both the drive to bond and the drive to acquire. Blake also had the added advantage that he was not exchanging time for money. Scale becomes much easier when you have a replicable product. Consider

254

the following as just a few of the things he did to get to the level of scale that quickly:

- He used social-networking sites such as Facebook, MySpace, Twitter, YouTube, and Flickr to make it easy for fans to spread the word.
- He hired interns for next to nothing who were part of the younger generation of hyper-connected consumers and had them spread the word.
- He asked everyone who bought a pair to help spread the word, which led to things such as restaurateurs having all their staff wear the shoes and then explaining why to their customers.
- He did as much media as he possibly could and got massive coverage, not just in print but TV as well. He was in *Time* magazine, *The New York Times* and *Men's Health,* just to name a few.
- He was featured in an AT&T ad. Blake obviously saw the appeal to a bigger company such as AT&T of being associated with such a positive story, and in turn Tom's Shoes got massive exposure from the campaign.
- He had Theory, the fashion label, build an entire campaign around its special Tom's Shoes range.
- He had Ralph Lauren, the legendary fashion designer, create a special line of Tom's Shoes.

The list could go on. What I would like to draw attention to now is the last two strategies above. When Blake tapped in to the retail network and brand power of Theory

255

and Ralph Lauren, he moved above the level of leverage and into the level of scale. Both had huge networks; both represented an opportunity for Tom's Shoes to benefit from the hard work of people not on Blake's payroll; and both gave him a return from a much bigger pie.

The key lesson here is that these opportunities opened up as a result of the coverage he got from the AT&T commercial he was in, which was aired America-wide. In other words, the AT&T experience bumped his brand into the world of "platform," and he was able to use this to get more leverage and more scale. Tom's Shoes was immediately thrust into the limelight and very quickly became a recognized brand in America.

A powerful and recognized brand gives you platform, and platform is where someone else can benefit from being associated with you—not just from on-selling your offer, as was the case with Bear Naked, but where just being able to say he or she is associated with you builds the power of that person's or company's brand. Platform gives you a license to do deals and to start relationships that give you leverage, scale and more platform simultaneously. Do this correctly and you will create a self-perpetuating cycle of bigger impact, more platform, bigger impact, more platform. Now, Blake is not at the movie-star level yet, where he can trade off the brand name alone (he still sells the shoes), but it is an example of the possibilities that can open up for you.

Dr. Stephen Covey is another great case in point. Covey is one of the most successful business authors and thought leaders of all time. He wrote the book *The Seven Habits of Highly Effective People*—a classic. Now, if you think about it, writing a book is a form of leverage, if you can sell enough copies. You write it once, and in Covey's case you sell the same book millions and millions of times (I wish). He also put it onto audio and spun more books out of the same ideas. He even decided at some later stage that there was an eighth habit. Needless to say, he copped a little bit of flak for that. He has since sold more than 20 million books and more than a million audio books.

Rather than make it all about him, Covey formed the Covey Leadership Center, which began by bringing on trainers who would teach others his methods and techniques. In time, this recruitment took on a much larger scale and became a licensing model, where people would effectively work for themselves using the Covey brand and course materials, and then the Covey Leadership Center would get a kickback every time they did a program or sold some materials.

Covey had his licensees go one step further. These trainers started licensing people within the client's company itself to deliver the programs more deeply and broadly in the same business. And every time they used Covey's materials, he would get a royalty as well as the profit margin that came from supplying the materials themselves. Most of these trainers and evangelists had never seen or met Stephen Covey but, because of the scale he has created, with their help his ideas were reaching millions of people all over the world.

Covey went one step further again when he merged the Covey Leadership Center with Franklin Quest to combine his perspectives on time management and prioritization with the actual tools to make it happen. Now he is

257

selling diaries, Outlook add-ins and dozens of different seminars and training products too.

Remember that he could have never done it if he had tried to control everything. At some point, if you want to move up the levels of impact you will need to give up trying to control everything. I personally have found this a major challenge in my professional life. As such, I have decided that acceleration is a journey of maturity!

One last thing, Covey's example represents the massive leverage and the massive scale he was able to get, but both came to him because he wrote such a great book (with great ideas), which then gave him the brand to build on. This brand was so powerful that companies would pay other people to teach them Covey's intellectual property—people who had never even met him. And that kind of brand power is what we call platform.

In much the same way that leverage comes from seizing the opportunities that present themselves to build your profile, platform is about seizing them consistently and then doing something with the results. Had Covey waited for a decade before trying to build the Covey Leadership Center, the momentum he had created with the publicity and buzz from the book would have dissipated and the opportunity would have passed him by. Now he has something enduring, because he had made hay while the sun shone.

Let's return to our Jerry Seinfeld example before moving on. With all the buzz and momentum that Jerry had built with his regular appearances on Letterman, and the great deal of trust he was building with producers and networks for his ability to engage an audience, he went to work on a sitcom of his own. He created a show called *The Seinfeld Chronicles*, which became the mammoth success and worldwide brand that we know today as Seinfeld. And, remember, this was on top of the packed theatres he was performing in for big fees and a percentage of the door-take. He was moving quickly up the five levels of impact.

Jerry's little show about nothing became the number-one sitcom in America within four years. Not being happy with that, and with his pedal still pushed to the metal, Seinfeld rehashed most of his old stand-up material into a book that fast became a *New York Times* bestseller.

By the eighth and ninth seasons of *Seinfeld*, he was also executive-producing the show and now, more than a decade after the last-made show went to air, the series is still syndicated and being watched all over the world. Not bad for a Jewish kid from New York whose father owned a sign company.

This, my friends, is what we call acceleration. You take whatever success you have had to date and you use it to further extend your reach. Every new step takes no more effort than the last—sometimes less—yet the return is always bigger. In Jerry's case, TV offered a bigger audience than stand-up; making his own show delivered greater returns than appearing on someone else's; producing offered greater returns again; oh, and his little bestseller that would have been pulled together with less work than the original stand-up routines that constituted it also would have delivered a very nice return.

259

All of these things firmly positioned Jerry Seinfeld on the right-hand side of the mental barrier. From there, he could do just about anything. He could reinvent himself in new and exciting ways, and do things he no doubt had always wanted to but likely had put on the back burner as he got sharp and compelling and propelled himself to that desirable side of the mental barrier.

With profile, you get platform. And with platform, you get permission—permission to try new things, to make different stuff happen.

MAKING ACCELERATION HAPPEN

▶ Learn to love your dissatisfaction and push on—there is always more on the table.

▶ Seek out and do the work to seize your moments of massive exposure.

▶ Deliberately pursue markets that have more lucrative buyers.

▶ Find out how you can bill for output (value) and not for inputs such as time.

▶ Leverage both mainstream media and new viral web 2.0 technology.

▶ Seek out large partners who have the distribution and relationships you need.

▶ Recruit followers, not just employees.

▶ Be prepared at times to give up some of the control to get the maximum scale possible.

▶ Consider what other brands and people have the exposure and recognition you need and align yourself with them.

▶ Build your brand so you can become the target partner or associate brand that others seek out.

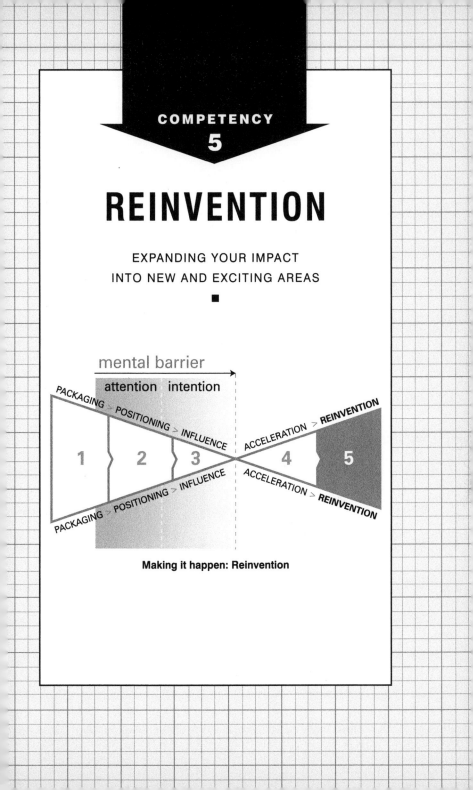

COMPETENCY
5

REINVENTION

EXPANDING YOUR IMPACT
INTO NEW AND EXCITING AREAS

■

mental barrier

attention   intention

PACKAGING > POSITIONING > INFLUENCE

ACCELERATION > REINVENTION

1   2   3   4   5

PACKAGING > POSITIONING > INFLUENCE

ACCELERATION > REINVENTION

Making it happen: Reinvention

15

YOU NEVER
REALLY "MAKE IT"

FOR ME, THIS is probably the chapter that comes most from the heart. When I first went on the journey to take what I had in my head and actually do something about it, I never believed for a moment that when I got it, I would be unfulfilled.

"If only I can be the general manager of the hotel, then my life will be perfect," I used to say.

And then, "If only I was working for myself, things would be better."

"If only I had 200 bookings a year instead of 100, then I would feel more secure," I said to myself next.

"If I can just buy a new BMW and have more than one house, then I really will be happy." It is all a big con. You will never be "happy" just because you have achieved what you so desired. It is a well-known fact, but you never believe that when you are on the journey, do you? When you are on the journey, you are so motivated, so juiced about making it happen that anyone who says it won't be all it is cracked up to be is automatically dismissed as never having been on a journey like the one you are on.

Well, I have, and I can tell you that when you get whatever you think you are after, it won't be enough either. Your drive to acquire will see to that. You can always be richer. You can always be more powerful. And you can always make a bigger contribution. The truth is, you feel most alive when you are in pursuit of something, not in possession of it. It turns out that striving to develop your idea, position it and influence people to engage with it is what brings you the most exciting times.

It is going through the process of making it happen that creates the joy and satisfaction that you crave, which ends up meaning one thing: if you want to live an enriching life, a life full of excitement, happiness and a sense of fulfillment, you have to constantly reinvent yourself. And I don't just mean reinvent yourself so you can sustain your financial success and stay on the cutting edge in your business; I mean reinvent yourself so you are still learning and growing.

The drives to comprehend, acquire, and bond are very powerful and healthy. The times in your life when you will feel lost are when you are desperately trying to hold on to what you have. The drive to defend, in my personal experience, is an empty one indeed. You see, you hold on so tightly to what you have achieved and created that you stop growing. You get so paranoid and so full of fear that you forget why you wanted all this in the first place. Whether it is power, whether it is money or whether it is just trying to hold on to the sense of purpose that your

266

work has brought you, it will ultimately feel empty after a time. We get bored. We need to move on.

I am the first to admit that getting started on the process of reinventing yourself is as difficult as inventing yourself for the first time. But the good news is that once you are started, it is easier. The only reason it is so difficult is that we are scared we won't be able to do it again. We are scared of all the work that goes into it. And we are scared that the end result will be nowhere near as fun as we first thought.

When you first got started, you probably felt as if you had so little to lose. Sure, you may have left your job, but you could always get another one. Sure, you may have had a mortgage, but your partner was working at the time so you knew it would be okay if things didn't work out. Now, based on your new, higher standards, reinventing yourself will frighten you to the core. At least, it did me.

This is perfectly normal, but it is no reason not to get moving. Plus, even though the fear makes it hard to get up and go again, you will be so much better at it this time.

The great irony is that you won't feel fully alive unless you start all over again. The model we have been working from tells you that you need to bond with new people, comprehend new things and acquire new experiences. It is as simple as that. And the sooner you see the signs and start the process, the better.

But that is much easier said than done. When I met Gary Kasparov, he called this the gravity of success. He said you get so weighed down by what you have achieved that you never move on to the next challenge. I wonder now whether he ever felt that ten chess championships would

267

be enough. He has since run for office in Russia to try to stamp out the corruption that is crippling that once-great nation, and I can only sense that he is feeling more alive than ever. Now, admittedly that might be because his life is in danger every day, but this is what it means to be a hero.

You are a hero. You have heard the call. In his great book, *The Hero with a Thousand Faces*, the famous mythologist Joseph Campbell talks about the hero's call. Every hero and heroine at some point in their journey hears the call. They know there is something great they must do. It usually requires coming face to face with their greatest fear, and conquering it. Well, isn't this what each of us are doing? You don't buy books like this unless you have already heard the call.

I would like to share with you something from my personal journey one last time. The other day, I was going through some old stuff in my home office and I stumbled across a poster-sized sheet of paper with a massive mind map on it. The paper was tatty and torn and had clearly been shoved under a pile of other junk for quite a few years. As it turned out, the mind map was my original vision for what my business would look like and what impact I would be able to make. It was bold for a 20-year-old, to say the least.

I had written down all sorts of aspirations on it. I wanted to change the way we taught in schools. I wanted to create a network of people creating positive change in the world. I wanted to give teenagers the tools they needed to be successful in the commercial worlds they were entering. I wanted to help organizations make their workplaces more inspiring through the adoption of much more open and collaborative cultures. And I wanted to make money doing all of these things.

At the time, it was pie in the sky, and I quickly realized that focus was far more important in these early days and that if I ever wanted the freedom to pursue these diverse goals I would need to focus first. That I did!

But when I look back on that mind map, some ten years on, I have achieved much of what is on it and more besides. And my business, the ChangeLabs, has been the vehicle.

A few years ago, I was working for a client on a financial-literacy event. I was to facilitate a dialogue between the media and other stakeholders on what the next generation thought about money and how we could best give them the skills they needed to effectively manage their money.

The client was the Commonwealth Bank Foundation, and this was just one of the many philanthropic initiatives they had going in an attempt to tool up the next generation of Australians. As it turned out, their largest program was underperforming, and they needed some help. And for me, this was one of those key moments that you can either let float by or grab with both hands.

I agreed to get involved, and in partnership with the foundation we have developed the largest face-to-face financial-literacy program of its kind in the world. The foundation's commitment to the cause and our expertise in creating powerful learning experiences came together, and the result is literally thousands of live sessions every year to well over 250,000 young people, teaching them valuable skills for their future.

With the success of this program, it was not long before we had developed programs with the likes of Apple and

269

IBM too. Now I have a business spread across the globe. But what is cool about it is that the very projects we run address the very desires I had expressed and had since completely forgotten about on my big mind map.

The coolest thing of all, though, was that I had been known for related but markedly different expertise, but through the trust I had developed with my clients I was able to reinvent myself in a way that had scale, leverage and more importantly made a positive difference in the world. It all happened so fast that I barely felt as if I had to work for it. And please don't read that last comment the wrong way. It offers powerful insight into why focus comes before freedom. When you are on the right side of the mental barrier, your impact is amplified and your progress accelerated. You can do far more far faster and far more easily than when you were getting started.

And the secret to reinvention is to get started while you are still on top.

TIMING IS EVERYTHING

It is never too early to start thinking about your reinvention. Never! Remember that, even with platform, your impact will dissipate over time. Now, this does not mean that you should abandon your progress on idea one and move to idea two—certainly not. But you can be laying the foundations of your next move while reaping the benefits of the first.

Have you noticed that things in life always take longer to get going than you anticipate, but that they gather momentum much faster than you thought? It is like we believe we can match our income in just a few months after leaving our jobs, only to find it really takes a year. Yet, in much the same way, we think it will be at least three years before we double it, and then it actually happens in 18 months. Things are slow at the start, and as such you need to begin your reinvention when you are at the height of your acceleration.

Reconsider the life-cycle concept we looked at earlier in the book. If you ignore the ultimate decline, it follows what is generally called an "S" curve. The same is true of your journey to make it happen. It will be like an S.

You will have to work extremely hard at first for little or no return. Then you get a breakthrough and acceleration rockets you up on a steep trajectory. But even though it won't feel like it while you are there, your rate of growth will slow. And the risk here is that you wait too long before launching the next idea that you want to turn into results. Don't let your life look like this:

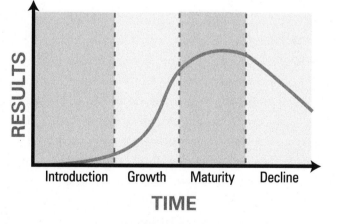

Life cycle of the offer

271

If, at the peak of your growth cycle, you were to start the process of reinvention, it would look like this:

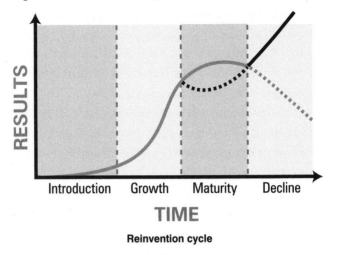

Reinvention cycle

The beauty of starting when your growth rate is at its peak is that when you reach the eventual maturity and decline of your initial idea, you will be on the way up again.

Now, a word of warning here. I say start early, but you need to be able to proceed without robbing your original idea of the focus and attention it deserves. Being an ideas person who never follows through is not your goal.

Yes, you want to start early, but you want to be certain that you are driving your stake deep where you are currently standing. You will feel invincible and ready to move on far earlier than your market has cemented your first offering in its mind, but you should wait until you have at least a couple of years of sustained success under your belt before you jump ship and get knee deep in your new idea.

Remember, the best marketing tool you have for sustained success, and subsequently what will give you the most trust among the buyers, is being really good at what you do. If your offer does indeed solve the problems and inspire the buyers in the way you suggested it would, fantastic, but it is pretty hard to get that good that fast.

So drive your stake deep, but don't get caught in the hole that you dig. To round out our exploration of Salesforce.com, consider that in the last few years, while they continue to grow at a rapid pace, they introduced a number of new offers to their market. A couple of examples include:

- **Chatter**—a social network for sales people designed to foster collaboration.
- **Force.com**—a "platform as a service" which allows third party developers to develop and sell add-ons that plug into the Salesforce.com infrastructure.

Now the truth be told, Chatter has not been a raging success for Salesforce.com because the general sense is it lacks some of the features and rigor that other similar cloud-based social networks offer. It is important to tread carefully with the "trust" you have built, as you don't want to find yourself killing your original success and momentum based on one additional offer which is not worthy of your brand.

What I love most about Salesforce.com though is how they have intertwined doing "good" into their business. They have built a very strong philanthropic offering, funneling profits from the business into important social causes. I bet Mark Benioff has long desired to make this

273

kind of impact, but there is no way he could have created as much positive social impact if he had not built the billion dollar juggernaut that is Salesforce.com. By staying focused with smart packaging, clearly moving a market to match his offer, structuring his offer in a way that made it very easy to buy, and accelerating its success through partnership, third party development, and the like he has truly made it happen. As promised, he has not cut off his options to make an impact in the social sphere, he has enhanced them because he has trust and he has results and he has the money.

16

STAGING YOUR REVOLUTION (OR EVOLUTION)

EVOLUTIONARY REINVENTION

Reinvention, in the sense in which I'm using it, does not have to be as radical as it might sound. You may not need to go in a completely new direction at all. In fact, if anything, it is more like a recalibration in reality. Examples of people who have completely reinvented themselves are few and far between. But you do need to chart a new path, and this can be so unsettling that it feels like a full reinvention. Generally, what you want to be doing is building on your existing capability before your expertise becomes redundant.

Allow me to explain. I once read a great line in a book by Jonas Ridderstrale and Kjell Nordstrom called *Funky Business* that said expertise is like milk, it goes off.

In other words, the skills you are mastering right now will one day be of no use to anyone. The same applies to the content matter you are becoming the go-to person for. In some technical disciplines, it is said that the half-life of what you learn at university is just four years. That means that half of what you learn in first year will be of no use to you when you graduate.

However, just because your expertise will go off, it does not mean that your capability will too. What sits below your content matter is a set of transferable abilities that can be of value in all sorts of different contexts. You may be an expert in law-firm business models, but over time you have shown yourself capable of transforming company cultures. You may have become an expert in adventure travel, but over time your capability is in structuring experiences that move people out of their comfort zone—whether through travel experiences or otherwise.

Build your reinvention from your capability!

IBM did this. A massive company, I know, but what it did was no less impressive. The transformation of IBM from primarily a hardware company to a professional-services firm is nothing short of brilliant. Don't get me wrong, IBM had for decades offered services and still manufactured hardware. Some of the great computer chips that power things such as the Xbox were developed by IBM. However, the powerhouse behind IBM today is the 175,000-person-strong consulting workforce, who do more than offer support for IT systems. IBM's transformation—aided by the acquisition of PricewaterhouseCoopers' consulting division—has helped to reposition IBM as

276

a strategic partner for the growth of its clients' businesses and for cost-cutting within those businesses. Not bad for a company that had seen its reputation dwindle to no more than the seller of technological hardware barely more than a decade ago.

Consider, in addition, Mark McCormack, the founder of IMG. It cracks me up how obvious certain things are in hindsight. I just can't believe there was no such thing as "managers" for sporting personalities until Mark McCormack founded IMG in 1960. But you needed to be there to know it was not really that obvious; it was just that McCormack saw a trend and an opportunity and seized it.

Mark McCormack was a good golfer, but not good enough. He qualified for the U.S. Open one year but did not make the cut. It obviously dawned on him that he was never really going to make it as a sports star, so he returned to his university qualification and began practicing again as a lawyer.

Staying in touch with his friends, some of whom were becoming very high-profile golfers indeed, he became the go-to guy for negotiating endorsement contracts. Many of his negotiations were carried out as a favor, but it got to a point when he realized there could be a business in this. Acting on the opportunity before him, he decided to start a business helping sporting figures manage their commercial relationships. What he had done was identify a trend. More and more sports were being televised, and McCormack saw the potential to leverage the growing celebrity of the players themselves.

277

To give you some insight into how early he was to pick up on and utilize this trend, consider that his first client was Arnold Palmer, followed by the likes of Gary Player, Jack Nicklaus, Björn Borg and Olympic skiing legend Jean-Claude Killy, just to name a few. And to underline how great his timing was, it was 1960 when he signed Palmer, who, in the next four seasons, won no fewer than 29 PGA Tour events.

It is so strange how one broken dream can lead to a new, even more exciting reality. What is interesting about the story of Mark McCormack is that even though he basically pioneered a whole new field, this was not for him that revolutionary. It was a natural extension of the skills and capabilities he had already built up. He was a good golfer and knew many of the players. He was also a good lawyer, and he could see that sport would become a powerhouse on commercial television.

I think of this as pushing your wedge further through the mental barrier.

Think about it: up until this point, I have told you to get sharper and sharper in your offering so you can get through the mental barrier, and I can't emphasize enough how important it is for you to do that. McCormack did this. IMG got started by his negotiating contracts specifically for golfers. However, before long he lined up a bulldozer and pushed his wedge so deep into the market that he and IMG became part of the fabric of sport as we know it today.

In the same way that TV viewers wanted to see their favorite stars on TV and brands could align themselves

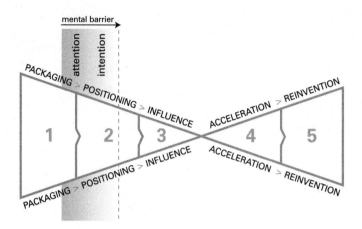

Making it happen: Pushing through

with this positive feeling through a paid endorsement, McCormack figured people would pay to meet these very same celebrities face to face. So he pioneered what we now think of as corporate hospitality. IMG went on to become the largest independent producer of sports content for television and the biggest licensor of rights.

Mark McCormack has been voted the most powerful man in golf, the most powerful man in tennis and then was named by *Sports Illustrated* as the most powerful man in sports.

What is especially interesting about the rise and rise of IMG is that every new wave was a logical extension of its predecessor. After becoming the principal manager of golf stars in a very short time, McCormack quickly moved to tennis—using the same skills, and the same corporate sponsors in some cases, too. Then,

279

instead of just representing the sports stars themselves, he saw an opportunity to manage the promoters of events and owners of teams as well. Wimbledon was one of his first clients, and at the time its name was being used all over the globe and it was getting no royalties for it at all. It seemed logical that he would manage the licensing of brand names in sport that were not the players themselves, so that's what he did.

And, of course, the process continued—new sports, new players, new opportunities. Every year saw a logical extension to what IMG was doing already. For example, sports stars were being approached about writing books, so IMG set up a literary agency.

Now, this story has a sad ending, with McCormack dying on the operating table before his time was up, but IMG itself remains the pre-eminent company in the world of sport. The company just keeps driving its wedge deeper. This capability and same-category-based reinvention is what I call "evolutionary reinvention."

REVOLUTIONARY REINVENTION

Not everyone is as single-minded as Mark McCormack. Richard Branson certainly is not. I know we have already discussed him in this book, but let me say quickly that when Branson wants to reinvent himself, he uses the already established assets of his personality, his eye for value and his ability to squeeze margins in a commodity business to take on a new industry. He is not always successful, for sure, but from music to trains, and from cola to planes, the Virgin empire keeps expanding, one reinvention at a time. Branson actually does this by partnering with people who have typically got more experience in this new field than he has himself, but they are revolutionary reinventions nonetheless.

So how might you go about completely reinventing yourself? Well, by starting from the beginning of this book and doing it all again—that's how. If your idea really is so left of field and so unrelated to your existing buyers and the trust and relationships you have built, then you need to start from square one.

The good news is that you will have built up some unbelievable experiences and will be able to go through it much faster than the first or the previous time you did.

At least, this is how it worked for three former employees of the payment-gateway giant PayPal. I want you to imagine that you have an idea for a video-sharing website. The time is the very beginning of the rebirth of the internet after the dot-com crash of 2001. How easy do you think it will be to get the venture-capital funding you will need to build a site this complex and pay for the bandwidth that would be required for video? My guess is not easy at all. That is unless, of course, you have a track record of being able to make it happen.

Chad Hurley, Jawed Karim, and Steve Chen were all very early employees of PayPal (which was actually a merger) and as such the 2002 sale to eBay would not only have been a big pay day for the boys (given the normal practice of giving stock options in return for lower salaries

281

in Silicon Valley start-ups) but also would have cemented their cred as people who knew how to build web properties that made money. Sure, they were not the founders, but they were a crucial part of the team.

So, for them, venture capital was nowhere near as difficult, because they had a well-packaged offer and they had trust. Their idea might have been completely unrelated to payment gateways, but it was good enough, and their credibility was well-established enough, to get the cash. Using an $11.5 million investment from Sequoia Capital, they went on their way to turning their idea for a video-sharing website into the reality of YouTube.

There are all sorts of great stories about the YouTube journey, including that its head offices were in a Japanese restaurant, but many of them are exaggerated. In short, they launched a beta version in mid-2005, took the site fully live in November 2005 and in less than 12 months sold the company for $1.65 billion in Google stock. I repeat, $1.65 billion! Just two years after that, it was ranked by Alexa Internet (a search-tracking company) as the fourth most-visited website in the world, behind Google, Yahoo, and Facebook.

Not bad for three young lads from Pennsylvania, Taiwan, and Germany. This is revolution of the most successful variety and shows just what can happen when you use the reputation you have built and the capability you have to master entirely new opportunities. And in YouTube's case, these were opportunities that no one had been able to exploit until then.

So, for one last example before we end our journey together, I want to talk about one of my favorite celebrity chefs: Jamie Oliver. Born into a publican family in England, a young Jamie Oliver struggled his way through school, suffering from dyslexia. After dropping out at 16 to do a course in catering, he eventually found himself working at The River Café, a well-known restaurant in Hammersmith, London. Someone from the BBC noticed this passionate young sous-chef, and before you know it he had his own show on the BBC. As a result of the three series and three specials that came from that show—*The Naked Chef*—Jamie went on to become a global TV star.

However, Oliver really showed his principles and character when, in spite of all his success and glamour, he decided to do something about the poor state of food in British schools. Using the platform he had created for himself, he launched a reinvention to change the way a country feeds its children. Sure, he used his strength (TV) and the brand it had afforded him, but this was a marked change from the light-hearted world of "how to cook a Sunday roast."

It was not a raging success by any stretch. He was widely criticized for taking himself too seriously, and the school students themselves even boycotted some of the healthier options presented to them in the schools the show was filmed in. But it did create change. More than 200,000 people signed a "Feed Me Better" petition, the then prime minister Tony Blair committed more funding and attention to the quality of food being served in British schools and local authorities began banning junk food in many of their schools.

283

It would be wrong to say he is now known for being a political activist, but what Oliver did was create genuine change in an area he was no doubt passionate about long before he got famous. As you well know, he is now taking on America, and having some success along the way.

MAKING REINVENTION HAPPEN

- ▶ Learn to love the gap between who you are and who you want to be, and realize you never really make it.

- ▶ Anticipate the need to reinvent or evolve long before it is essential to do so, and look forward to beginning the process with greater trust in the minds of your new buyers.

- ▶ Leverage off your momentum and success and start reinventing right when you are at the top of your game.

- ▶ Don't get fat and lazy and bogged down by the gravity of your success. Remember, the world needs people like you who know how to make it happen.

- ▶ Keep your eyes open. Opportunity is everywhere.

Conclusion

GO AND MAKE IT HAPPEN

I HAVE WRITTEN this book for myself as much as for anyone else. I wanted to remind myself to ante up again, to get back in the game and play another hand. I was reminding myself just as much as you that just because we are already successful in our life, whatever that means for us, we should not stop. I walk around in the post-global¬financial-crisis world, and I see people without a purpose and without a sense of direction.

If I made $100 for every executive I have met who has lost the spark in his or her eyes, I would have enough money to buy some of these people's companies. For you, the reinvention may be what you do after your career. It may be that you are moving into what has become known as the "third phase." Like retirement was ever going to stop you. Fancy packing up your bat and ball at 60-odd and going home. You have just spent the best part of your life developing the wisdom and the relationships to be able to make a massive impact. What you can do with that knowledge is extraordinary. I know deep down that you have heard that call too.

As for my own generation, Generation Y, this is now a time to lead. With our older siblings moving into senior roles, we will be called upon to make it happen. I feel at some level that our whole generation has heard the call, and that is why we have proven so challenging to employ in old-school jobs in companies with practices that date back to the middle of the last century. Let's put our money where our mouths are and start creating the results we constantly talk about achieving.

So, as you step into the breach again, my dear friends, let me share with you my final outline for making it happen:

- Package your aspiration as an offer that someone can buy.
- Position your offer to a market need and make sure it is sharp and compelling.
- Influence buyers to commit by understanding how your offer will enhance the way they see themselves and satisfy the drives that churn inside them.
- When you get some momentum, put your foot on the accelerator and seize the key moments that present themselves to get leverage and scale your results.
- And, just when you think you are on fire, start laying the foundations for your next project.

288

Every day, you hear stories of success, of people who have gone out and made it happen. There is absolutely no reason on earth why this cannot be you. You are ten times smarter and ten times more capable than you think you are. Now that you have the strategies, you need to act on them.

So, stop reading and go and make it happen!

ACKNOWLEDGMENTS

First and foremost, I would like to thank my wife, Sharon. Books take three times longer and are five times more stressful to write than you imagine. Sharon kept me on track, brought me coffee on the jet-lagged mornings, chicken soup on the flu-ridden days just short of deadline and basically reminded me it was worth the effort. She is the rock on which all our shared success is built.

My heartfelt thanks and appreciation also go to the following people:

To everyone who read and offered feedback on the book.

To Rae Lee Olson, for invaluable insight into structure and expression and for getting up at 3 a.m. on her Hawaii vacation to get it done. Rae Lee, your and Karl's support and friendship on our American journey has been invaluable to Sharon and me. Thank you both so much.

To Dom Thurbon, who was instrumental in the early days, shaping the ideas that underpin this book. Dude, you have become a force of nature when it comes to making it happen. You know how to get it done. I am personally forever in your debt. And to think we are just getting started.

To Matt Church. As always, you are my brother on this journey. Love you, man.

To Dave Willis, who had the courage to tell me what was really wrong with the early manuscript and give it to me straight. Only a real friend would be that straight.

To Joe Calloway, who was busy penning his own bestseller yet still found the time to offer his insight. Joe, you inspire me more than you know.

To Phill Nosworthy, who read and reread the manuscript, sharpening its edges and telling me what worked. You are a king, no question. A rain-maker, no less.

To Hendo, Zey, Sasha, Chantelle, and Mandy, whose feedback was extremely helpful.

To John Hellerman and Sheryle Moon for the countless suggestions and case studies to support my perspectives.

To Emma Hogan, who has been my go-to person for years on all things personal-brand and book related. You really are a great friend.

To Dean "Pedro" McEvoy. Pedro, the work we did that week in LA has had a profound impact on my business. Thanks, mate.

To Simon Breakspear and Dale Beaumont. Your help around titles and positioning at the eleventh hour was a lifesaver. Thanks, boys.

To my little sister, Jen, who has become a designer extraordinaire. The mental models look great and I love the cover!

And to Mary Cunnane and Marcus Hoffman. We are forming quite a team these days. I am very lucky to have you, and thanks for your patience.

And to my new team at BenBella Books. Congratulations on your own journey in a highly competitive industry. You are making it happen. Most of all, thanks for believing in me. Fingers crossed.

ACKNOWLEDGMENTS

WORKS CITED

Ariely, Dan, *Predictably Irrational: The Hidden Forces that Shape our Decisions*, New York, Harper, 2008

Campbell, Joseph, *The Hero with a Thousand Faces*, Princeton, New Jersey, Princeton University Press, 1949

Caples, John, *Tested Advertising Methods*, Englewood Cliffs, New Jersey, Prentice-Hall, 1974

Colvin, Geoff, *Talent is Overrated: What Really Separates World-Class Performers from Everybody Else*, London, Portfolio, 2008

Covey, Stephen R., *The Seven Habits of Highly Effective People: Restoring the Character Ethic*, Melbourne, Business Library, 1990

Galeano, Eduardo, *Open Veins of Latin America: Five Centuries of the Pillage of a Continent*, Cedric Belfrage (trans.), New York, Monthly Review Press, 1973

Gilbert, Daniel, *Stumbling on Happiness*, London, HarperCollins, 2006

Gladwell, Malcolm, *Blink: The Power of Thinking Without Thinking*, New York, Little, Brown and Co., 2005 *Outliers: The Story of Success*, Melbourne, Allen Lane, 2008 *The Tipping Point: How Little Things Can Make a Big Difference*, New York, Little, Brown and Co., 2000

Harford, Tim, *The Undercover Economist*, New York, Random House, 2005

Lawrence, Dr P. R., and Nitin Nohria, *Driven: How Human Nature Shapes our Choices*, San Francisco, Jossey-Bass, 2002

Levitt, Steven, and Stephen J. Dubner, *Freakonomics: A Rogue Economist Explores the Hidden Side of Everything*, London, Allen Lane, 2005

Ridderstrale, Jonas and Kjell Nordstrom, *Funky Business: Talent Makes Capital Dance*, London, BookHouse Publishing, 2000

Sheahan, Peter, *Flip: How Counter-Intuitive Thinking is Changing Everything – From Branding and Strategy to Technology and Talent*, Sydney, Random House Australia, 2007 *Generation Y: Thriving and Surviving with Generation Y at Work*, Melbourne, Hardie Grant, 2005

Weiss, Alan, *Million Dollar Consulting: The Professional's Guide to Growing a Practice*, New York, McGraw-Hill, 1992